Stress

ISSUES FOR THE NINETIES

Volume 32

Editor

Craig Donnellan

Independence
Educational Publishers
Cambridge

First published by Independence
PO Box 295
Cambridge CB1 3XP

© Craig Donnellan 1997

Copyright
This book is sold subject to the condition that it shall not,
by way of trade or otherwise, be lent, resold, hired out or otherwise
circulated in any form of binding or cover other than that in which it
is published without the publisher's prior consent.

Photocopy licence
The material in this book is protected by copyright. However, the
purchaser is free to make multiple copies of particular articles for instructional
purposes for immediate use within the purchasing institution.
Making copies of the entire book is not permitted.

British Library Cataloguing in Publication Data
Stress – (Issues for the Nineties Series)
I. Donnellan, Craig II. Series
155.9'042

ISBN 1 86168 023 6

Printed in Great Britain
City Print Ltd
Milton Keynes

Typeset by
Claire Boyd

Cover
The illustration on the front cover is by
Andrew Smith/Folio Collective.

CONTENTS

Chapter One: Young people and stress

Mental health and young people	1
Stressed out	3
Exams make teenagers suicidal	5
I nearly cracked up	6
How to cope with the stress of student life	8
The feel-bad factor	9
Are you worried? Are you under stress?	11

Chapter Two: Stress at work

Stress at work	12
Stress in the workplace	14
How stress at work could be shrinking your brain	16
Managing stress	17
Are managers under stress?	18
Why stress is breeding the office superbully	20
Workplace bullying may cost employers and state £12 billion a year	21
The cost of stress	22

The legal position	23

Chapter Three: Coping with stress

What makes you angry?	24
20 sure-fire stress beaters	26
Lie back and enjoy your vices, say scientists	29
A little of what you fancy . . .	29
Stress – why does it happen?	30
Time to talk	31
Changing your life	32
Anxiety and depression quiz	33
Anti-stress room is a smash hit	34
Help! I haven't got time for my life	35
Phoney smile at work will end in tears	37
Index	38
Additional resources	39
Acknowledgements	40

Introduction

Stress is the thirty-second volume in the series: **Issues For The Nineties**. The aim of this series is to offer up-to-date information about important issues in our world.

Stress looks at young people and stress, stress in the workplace and ways of coping with stress.

The information comes from a wide variety of sources and includes:
Government reports and statistics
Newspaper reports and features
Magazine articles and surveys
Literature from lobby groups
and charitable organisations.

It is hoped that, as you read about the many aspects of the issues explored in this book, you will critically evaluate the information presented. It is important that you decide whether you are being presented with facts or opinions. Does the writer give a biased or an unbiased report? If an opinion is being expressed, do you agree with the writer?

Stress offers a useful starting-point for those who need convenient access to information about the many issues involved. However, it is only a starting-point. At the back of the book is a list of organisations which you may want to contact for further information.

*****

CHAPTER ONE: YOUNG PEOPLE AND STRESS

Mental health and young people

Attitudes and awareness among 11-24 year-olds

Today's young people are very concerned about the state of the world in which we live, and within which they will soon be expected to function as responsible adults. Notably, 21 per cent of respondents were concerned about the effects of pollution on their lives. Crime levels within the area in which they and their families live was also of great concern, as was the cost of living, unemployment, money and education.

Only a tiny minority (1 per cent) of respondents expressed concern about having a partner, girl or boyfriend, perhaps reflecting the changing state of adolescence and young adulthood in the late twentieth century. Of all those questioned, it was the younger adolescents who seemed more concerned about being in a couple. While problem pages still devote a lot of space to matters of the heart, it is the case that an agony aunt's postbag contains more and more letters concerning a wide variety of issues. And while romance remains very important, it seems to be increasingly overshadowed by other concerns such as money, family, and the environment. Young people are also acutely aware of the implications of failing their exams in terms of their future prospects.

Young people's aspirations seem to centre around money, education and employment – with consequent problems when their aspirations are not matched by opportunities. In response to being asked what would need to change or happen in order to improve their quality of life, good or better employment opportunities were considered by 22 per cent to be a significant factor. Financial security was felt by 21 per cent of respondents to be the answer to their problems, with improved academic performance the key factor for 10 per cent. Interestingly, sex and the need for a partner were seen by only 1 per cent of respondents to be necessary for improving their quality of life.

> **Concerns**
>
> What do young people worry about and how might they improve the quality of their lives?
>
> *'I'd like not to worry so much about my work.'*
> (20 year old C1 female)
>
> *'I think I'd be happier if I lost a bit of weight.'*
> (15 year old DE female)
>
> *'I want to get a job and not waste so much money on drink.'*
> (19 year old DE male)
>
> *'We need to make the world a better place by getting rid of pollution and protecting the animals that might be extinct.'*
> (15 year old AB female)

Coping

Positive steps today

The research found that listening to music was by far the most popular and relied upon method for coping with stress – a finding which might please DJs rather more than health professionals. Four out of five young people felt that listening to music was the most helpful way of dealing with problems on a daily basis. In addition, a third of all respondents found listening to music particularly useful in helping to prevent future stress and anxiety. As music can be made fairly accessible to most young people, this may be relevant to both parents and professionals who have in the past criticised either the volume or choice of music made by young people. Music brings people together and can also be used to help express or come to terms with difficult feelings.

About 60 per cent of those questioned said they would approach a female friend or relative for advice and support with problems. The same number found that going out with friends or family helped them to manage their problems effectively. Although 48 per cent of young men will discuss problems with a male friend and 38 per cent with a male relative, in general young men prefer doing to talking. For example, 35 per cent of males as opposed to 25 per cent of females used regular exercise as a way to de-stress. Twenty-one per cent of young men in their late teens and early twenties went to the pub to help forget their troubles, while only 15 per cent of young women felt this was a solution.

Young women were much more likely to find support by talking about their problems. In particular, 71 per cent of the younger female respondents said they would turn to a female relative or friend for support, while 48 per cent of those aged 19 would do the same. Almost a quarter of all those questioned had approached a GP for help, with 89 per cent of those finding it useful. In addition, 35 per cent of female respondents have sought help from a counsellor or an advice organisation as opposed to 28 per cent of males. Young women were also more likely to seek help from magazines or books, perhaps reflecting the fact that while there is a well-established medium for young women to explore emotional issues, few equivalent media exist for young men. Some magazines targeting young men have, perhaps, been slow to discuss such concerns, while the recent emergence of 'laddish' titles has marked a shift away from exploring these issues.

Positive steps tomorrow

Today's young people will continue to look for support and guidance from family and friends to help them cope with stress. More than half said they would share their problems with a female relative or friend, while less than half said they would turn to a male friend or relative. Thirteen per cent said they would approach a neighbour for help or advice, and 6 per cent said they would consider using the internet – compared with 2 per cent who currently do.

Listening to music was felt by 35 per cent of respondents to be a helpful long-term way of avoiding stress or anxiety. Working harder, taking exercise, resting and seeking advice from a counsellor were considered by more than a quarter to be things which could be effective and/or helpful in managing problems and stress.

Only 5 per cent of all the young people surveyed considered regular trips to the pub and/or having an alcoholic drink to be useful in preventing future problems. An even smaller number (4 per cent) of respondents smoked more when besieged by worries, and 2 per cent (mainly females) ate more when they felt upset. In addition, only 2 per cent of the adolescents and young people involved in this survey choose to seek solace in drugs when trying to cope with or escape from their problems. Of those who did use drugs, 98 per cent acknowledged that in the long term drugs provided no positive rewards or benefits in really coming to terms with problems and anxieties.

It is worth noting that young people have their own vocabulary to articulate the kind of feelings that health professionals describe as 'mental health problems'. Many of those questioned, however, are actively finding positive, non-destructive ways of coping with their problems. Letters to teenage magazines seem to show that in many cases, young people will attempt to discuss problems before doing something about them. They need to have a safe place where they can think through their concerns as well as needing a trusted source of support in whom they can confide.

• This research was carried out for the Health Education Authority by Research and Auditing Services (RAS) to mark World Mental Health Day 1996. RAS carried out 1,853 30-minute interviews with young people aged 11 to 24 throughout England. Of those questioned, 48 per cent were male and 52 per cent female. Ten per cent of those interviewed were from ethnic minorities.

© *Health Education Authority*
October, 1996

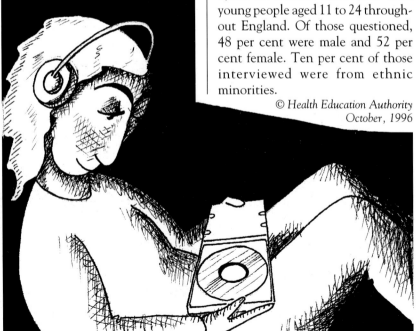

Stressed out

What children tell ChildLine about exams and work pressure

Introduction

'It all feels out of control . . . I'm so stressed out . . . I've got too much to do . . . I can't cope with the pressure.'

The significance of the world of school in children's lives can hardly be overstated. They spend the majority of each day in school. Their friendships are made and broken there; or, if they cannot find friends, they feel the effects of loneliness and isolation. There they learn how to be social creatures, absorbing the rules and conventions of the cultures they inhabit; they develop the peer relationships which have such importance in how they feel about themselves and others, and how they feel it is right to behave; and, there, they prepare for and take the national examinations which can determine how their future careers will develop.

So it is not surprising that ChildLine hears from so many children about difficulties in their school lives. In the year up to 31 March 1995, we heard from 4139 children about problems within school.

Among the most poignant of these are the calls from children about exam and work pressures. These are youngsters who feel they are failing themselves, their parents and their schools.

Mark had his A level exams the following week. He said:

'Everything seems to be going wrong for me.' He was in tears as he talked about the high expectations his parents had of him, including going to university, and his fears that he would fail and let them down. He felt he could not tell his parents how he felt, because he believed that they would be disappointed in him. He had tried to talk to a teacher, but had not been able to say how he really felt.

ChildLine school questionnaire

In 1994/95 ChildLine counselled 90,200 children and young people who contacted us for the first time that year. Of these, 17,004 (19%) were children and young people experiencing problems at school.

One of the questions asked by the survey was which problems young people worried about the most. Children were offered 12 boxes to tick and asked to tick as many as they wanted. The choices were: problems at home, schoolwork/exams, how they looked, bullying, parents divorcing or separating, sex, relationships with friends, being followed or attacked, being hit, being abused, the environment, and their future.

Their responses showed unequivocally that children and young people worry more about schoolwork and exams than anything else in their lives – 79 per cent of the 1022 respondents to this question indicated that schoolwork/exams was a worry; 66 per cent worried about their future; next came being followed or attacked, a worry for 46 per cent of children – especially for boys; problems at home worried 44 per cent of children. Thirty-six per cent mentioned bullying. These percentages do not add up to 100 because children ticked more than one box – an average of four for each respondent.

Age of callers

Fear of exams was the main reason for calling in 96 of the cases examined. The majority of these callers were aged 14 (13.5%), 15 (41.6%) and 16 (21.8%). Some younger children were also worried about exams, the youngest being 11 years old, and as SATS and league tables are fully established we expect to hear from more of the younger age group. In some instances younger children were concerned about exams several years in the future, already felt pressure to do well and were afraid of failure. The ratio of girls to boys in these calls was just under three to one. The average ratio

Calls about exam stress (as %)								
Age	11	12	13	14	15	16	17	Not known
Girls	0.0	4.1	4.1	10.4	29.1	17.7	1.1	4.1
Boys	1.0	2.0	2.0	3.1	12.5	4.1	1.0	0.0
Total	1.0	6.1	6.1	13.5	41.6	21.8	5.1	4.1

Calls about work pressure (as %)									
Age	7-10	11	12	13	14	15	16	17-18	Not known
Girls	1.8	2.4	6.6	13.8	16.8	14.4	10.8	3.6	9.6
Boys	0.6	1.2	0.0	1.8	6.6	4.2	2.4	1.2	1.8
Total	2.4	3.6	6.6	15.6	23.4	18.6	13.2	4.8	11.4

of girls to boys for calls to ChildLine is four to one.

One hundred and sixty-six callers, many of whom were experiencing profound distress, talked about having difficulties with schoolwork. Sixty-six of these callers had called about exam pressure, but also needed to talk about more generalised pressures of work. The majority of these calls were from 13- to 16-year-olds. The youngest caller was only seven years old, and the oldest 18. The ratio of girls to boys in these calls was four to one.

The calls

As children move through their school careers, and GCSEs and A-levels approach (Standard Grades and Highers in Scotland), they begin to have to deal not only with the demands of an increasing workload, but also need to make choices and decisions which may affect the course of their lives for many years ahead.

By striving to do their best, many young people achieve the goals which they and their families wish for. Doing well in examinations can bring great opportunities for the future, and gives children a sense of positive self-worth and satisfaction through achievement. But it is also a time when some children begin to fail to reach the goals set for them, or experience great pressure in reaching them. As well as being able to attain the rewards of academic success, some will have to confront the possibility of failure.

It should also be remembered that school does not exist in isolation from the other parts of young people's lives. The problems they talked about to the counsellors at ChildLine were often complex, and the pressures at school were often associated with other difficulties in their lives. Problems at home, such as parents splitting up or unsatisfactory parent–child relationships, changing schools, illness, bereavement, and learning or behavioural difficulties were part of the picture for many of the children who called ChildLine about school problems. Because most of these children were aged between 13 and 16, they were also at a stage in their lives when they were having to deal with all the uncertainties,

> 'Everyone expects too much of me.'
>
> 'I'm just stupid and abnormal.'
>
> 'Mum and Dad just don't realise I'm not as clever as my brother.'
>
> 'I know I need to work . . . I just can't motivate myself.'
>
> 'I just feel tired . . . I've got no time, no motivation, no rewards.'
>
> 'I feel stuck, as though there's no way out.'

changes and vulnerability of adolescence.

It is to be expected that children will experience pressure at this time. But for the children who spoke to ChildLine counsellors about exams and schoolwork, the pressure had become unbearable, and many felt that their whole future hung in the balance. They described feeling out of control, panic-stricken, over-burdened and overwhelmed, often saying they could not cope any more and, occasionally, they were suicidal. Many said that they had little support and that they felt unable to confide in those around them.

The pressures

Parents want their child to do well at school, and view good exam results as a way of opening doors to a successful and secure future for their child. Indeed, children very much need the support and encouragement of their parents at this time of great pressure. One of the biggest problems facing parents, and also teachers, is how to give support and encourage-ment in a way that doesn't put unreasonable pressure on the child.

Many of the children who called about work and exam stress felt that the expectations placed on them by their parents to do well in exams, or with their schoolwork, were too high or unrealistic. In some instances the parents had made their expectations clear to the child in a very direct way, for example, by setting specific goals for the child.

A 15-year-old girl was extremely distressed, and cried throughout the 30-minute call. She was doing nine GCSEs and also worked at a part-time job. She said her mum had very high standards, and nagged her continually about her work, expecting her to get straight As. She had already decided on her future university course, and her mother had said that if she didn't get the grades to get on that course, she would have to leave home. She was feeling so stressed

Exams make teenagers suicidal

By Peter Victor

Children as young as seven are so stressed by school work and exams that some of them consider suicide, according to a report published today.

Mounting pressure for academic success has made school work the number one worry in children's lives.

A survey report entitled *Stressed Out*, which was produced for the charity ChildLine, pinpoints parental pressure fears about the future and the lack of anyone to talk to as key sources of stress among pupils.

The majority of children who called the charity's helpline in distress over their schoolwork were aged 14 to 16, but ChildLine has had calls from some pupils as young as 12 who were already afraid of not getting into university. The youngest caller was seven.

One girl, called Susie, tried to hang herself because of the pressure of GCSEs before ringing ChildLine last year. Others were in tears when they called, many had played truant to avoid stressful work and 13 said they were contemplating suicide.

More than 1.25 million pupils are preparing to sit exams this summer. Of the 17,004 children who called ChildLine about problems with school in 1994-95, just 196 were primarily concerned about work and exams – far fewer than for bullying, abuse or relationships.

A survey of 1,000 children carried out for the report found that 79 per cent worried about exams and schoolwork 'more than anything else in their lives'. John Hall, the report's author, said the figures suggest many children are able to cope with exam pressures with the help of friends,

> **Mounting pressure for academic success has made school work the number one worry in children's lives**

teachers and parents. But he added: 'The children who call ChildLine are the ones who feel unable to share their worries with anyone else or who have tried and found their listeners unsympathetic.

'These are children for whom the pressure has become unbearable, and many feel their whole future hangs in the balance. They describe feeling out of control, panic-stricken, over-burdened and overwhelmed, often saying that they have little support and that they feel unable to confide in those around them.'

Parents with high expectations can make matters worse when what they see as encouragement is interpreted by the child as yet more pressure to succeed.

One tearful 15-year-old girl told ChildLine that her mother had told her she would have to leave home if she failed to get straight A grades in her GCSEs.

Others said their parents put pressure on them to achieve what they themselves had failed to achieve at school.

© *The Independent*
April, 1996

---

that she was not eating, and wanted to go to the doctor for tranquillisers.

In other calls high expectations were communicated less directly, and pressure arose from children feeling that they had to do as well as a more successful sibling, or pass exams that a parent had never had the opportunity to take.

A 13-year-old with end of year exams approaching felt that no matter how well he did, his parents felt it was never good enough. He said his father and older sister were very bright, and this was hard to live up to. He also said his mum put him under pressure to achieve what she herself had failed to achieve at school, and that when he had told his parents that he didn't want to go to university, they 'had gone mad'.

A 16-year-old girl was under great pressure from her father to do well in A levels the following year. He was paying for a private tutor, but she felt panicked and was having trouble concentrating. She said: 'I am not on target to do as well as they want.' She said her dad had no education and told her that she would 'end up on the dole queue' if she didn't succeed at school.

There was mention in a very few calls that children also felt pressed to do well for the school's sake, as schools want to do well in examination result league tables. However, there is insufficient evidence from our sample to say categorically whether league tables are increasing the pressure on children, although, given the level of anxiety they already

experience, it would be surprising if this were not the case.

• The above is an extract from *Stressed Out*, a ChildLine study. It is based on an in-depth examination os calls from 196 young people whose *main problem* was work and exam pressure. ChildLine is the free national help-line for children and young people in trouble and danger. It provides a confidential telephone counselling service for any child with any problem, 24 hours a day, every day. Trained counsellors provide support and advice and refer children in danger to appropriate helping agencies. Children can phone ChildLine on 0800 1111 or write to ChildLine, Freepost 1111, London N1 0QW.   © *ChildLine*

I nearly cracked up

Mandy's parents demanded a lot. And then there were the problems with friends at school. The pressure was building up and she just knew she was about to crack...

My parents have always had high hopes for me – maybe too high. From the second I walked through the school gates to start my first GCSE year, they were on my back about 'getting into good habits early on' and 'doing that little bit extra' when it came to homework.

At first I brushed their comments aside. I'd always tried hard at school, anyway For as long as I could remember, I've always dreamed of becoming a vet. But I soon realised Mum and Dad expected a much higher standard from me and I just wasn't sure I could give it to them.

Unlike some of my brainy friends, I had to do twice the studying they did to get good marks. Before my final GCSE year, that had meant the odd late night and a bit of extra help around exam time. But things changed dramatically once I was in the fifth form.

The first warning sign was maths. I was in the top class the year before, but after a couple of months I was really struggling. Some nights I had to spend up to three hours studying just to get through my maths homework. The frustrating thing was, that when it came to history, English and art, I passed with my eyes shut.

By the time the mock maths exam came around, I'd worked myself into a real state. I'd bitten my nails so badly I had to wear plasters. Worse still, I'd drunk so much coffee the night before the exam that when I finally got to bed, I tossed and turned for hours.

Waiting outside the classroom before the exam, I remember all my mates chatting away saying things like, 'I haven't revised enough for this exam – I know I'm gonna fail.' But I *had* revised and I was still sure I'd fail.

Not good enough

A few days later I found out I'd passed the maths exam by just three marks. I could hardly contain my joy! But when I broke the good news to Mum and Dad, they weren't as happy as I'd imagined.

> *By the time the mock maths exam came around, I'd worked myself into a real state. I'd bitten my nails so badly I had to wear plasters*

'Hmmm... we'll have to get you a tutor,' Dad muttered, hardly disguising his feelings. 'A tutor?' I yelled. I couldn't believe it.

'It's for your own good, Mandy,' added Mum. 'You're obviously not mathematically inclined and you don't want to fail, do you?'

Well I felt like a failure then. Hadn't they seen how hard I'd studied? I lay crying myself to sleep that night, as I realised that I'd never be what they wanted me to be.

The crunch

Exams and homework were causing me enough grief, but I soon had more stress to deal with. Sally, the most popular girl in our group, really fancied this lad in the next form. But my best friend, Carrie, ended up getting off with him at a party. It got back to Sally and Carrie wrongly assumed that I'd been the one who'd told her. I had a massive row with Carrie and she stopped speaking to me!

Over the next few weeks, I was given the silent treatment – not only by Carrie but everyone else in our group! I was so depressed I didn't know where to turn. Lunch times became unbearable and I would often end up crying tears of frustration – unable to get anyone to hear my side of the story.

After about two weeks of this, I finally rang Carrie to apologise for whatever it was that I was meant to have done, but she simply said, 'Yeah, OK.' She didn't really talk to me at all.

That night I lay in bed crying again for what seemed like hours and hours. When daylight started to creep through my curtains I realised I'd spent the whole night wide awake. I tried to get up in the morning but I just didn't have the will to move.

Breaking point

I ended up spending the whole day just curled up in bed. The only time I got out was to go to the loo. I didn't eat or sleep, I just lay there – a million ridiculous thoughts whizzing through my brain. Unbelievably, nobody noticed. I usually got myself off to school in the mornings because Mum and Dad both left for work before me, so no-one twigged that I spent the day in bed. When Mum came home I said I had a migraine and wanted to be left alone.

The next day I dragged myself into school – afraid that if I missed another day I'd never catch up. Towards the end of maths, my teacher, Ms Rogers, tapped me on the shoulder and said, 'Can I have a word after class, Mandy?'

As I approached her desk my heart started beating wildly.

Shuffling some papers, she said, 'I'm a bit worried about you. I know you did OK in your maths exam, but you've been looking tired and stressed. Can I do anything to help?'

I tried to hold back the tears, but before I knew it I was a blubbering mess. Ms Rogers just handed me tissue after tissue as I poured out how worried I was and how hard I was finding everything.

'Do your parents know how you feel, Mandy?'

'Yes!!' I snivelled. 'But they think I'm not trying hard enough.'

'I think I get the picture,' she said finally.

Stress control

Looking back, the solution was so easy! I don't know why I didn't drop to a lower maths class sooner. Ms Rogers rang Mum and explained that it was no use getting me a tutor when I was clearly struggling.

Dropping down made such a difference! The lower maths class was easier (I'd already done most of the work) and I did better in my other subjects because I was less stressed out.

Things with my crowd got better, too. Carrie stopped being so nasty and the whole thing died down as quickly as it had started.

When my GCSE results came through I knew I'd done the right thing. I got four Bs and an incredible three As – and one of them was in maths! I got a C in geography, but even Dad understood that!

© *Sugar*

How do you chill out?

We hit the streets to find out how you cope when the pressures of the world are getting too much! Most of you seem to believe in talking it out with someone. Well, they do say a problem shared is a problem halved!

'If I'm feeling down about something, then I go and eat chocolate – it always makes me feel better! I put myself under a lot of pressure waiting for my exam results, but by worrying so much I made it much worse for myself.'
Louise Oldman, 18

'If I'm stressed out, I talk to my best friend. I'll go round to her house in tears and she'll give me a big hug! It makes me feel better when I've got her to talk to.'
Celia Hollands, 18

'If a really bad problem is stressing me out, I talk to my mum. We get on really well and she always makes me feel better. When I was taking my A-levels I had to make sure I kept having breaks and getting out of the house.'
Kelly Harris, 18

'I talk to my best friend when I'm under pressure, I think that's better than keeping it to yourself.'
Pinar Kemal, 17

'When I'm stressed, I like to listen to music. I try and sort out the problem in my own head rather than talking to anyone else. Listening to my favourite songs helps me put everything into perspective.'
Helen Blumfield, 18

'I phone my older sister when I'm under stress. She's really good at helping me with my problems. I'm lucky because I don't get stressed very often. I try not to let things worry me too much.'
Zoe Peirce, 19

'I get stressed out with my parents, but I try to stay calm and explain my point of view to them. I get a better result if I don't get too upset with them.'
Dhara Patel, 17

© *Sugar*

How to cope with the stress of student life

Information from MIND

Student life can be stressful. It is a transitional period: you do a course because you think it will enable you to do or have something that you want, such as increased job opportunities or enhanced enjoyment of life. Studying is part of a process of change. Student life is also very pressured: a lot has to be achieved in the limited time available. All this can be exciting, but it can also cause anxiety. This article will focus on some of the anxieties you are likely to encounter as you embark on your student years and suggest ways of coping.

Leaving home – what difficulties should I expect?

If you go to university straight from school, you are facing the challenge of leaving home, separating from your parents and beginning the process of finding your identity as an adult and your place in the world. This is a big psychological upheaval, but it also involves many challenges at a practical level: you will need to practise housekeeping, managing a budget and finding your way around a strange place. This all demands energy, just as you are beginning to take on the work requirements of your course and build a social life.

Mature students

Mature students will already have left home, but will still have many changes to deal with. There may be less money, less free time, and a change in social status, for better or worse. You may have children and a partner: your new life will have an impact on them, and your relationship with them will be affected.

Changing identity

You may go from being a biggish fish in a smallish pond (as a sixth former at school, or manager in a company) to being a tiny fish in an enormous pond. You may feel differently about yourself, and other people may react to you differently. You will be making new friends, and have a chance to make a fresh start. You may be working with peers who are your intellectual equals for the first time in your life; you may find you are cleverer than, or not so clever as, you had thought. It takes time to adjust to this new sense of who you are.

New opportunities

There may be sports, social and political activities open to you now, which you've never tried before. This has two aspects: it can be very exciting, but it can also be terrifying. Don't get swept away! It would be unwise to go on your first potholing expedition, for example, on the same weekend that you are moving into new lodgings and handing in your first essay! Recognise how much you are dealing with at once, and go at your own pace. Be prepared to feel terrified sometimes.

Family relationships

Relationships with your family will change too. This can be especially difficult if you are the first one ever to go to college, or the first of your gender. Other family members can have complicated feelings about this: they may secretly envy you, or be afraid that your new experience will make you too strange and hard to communicate with – no longer 'one of us'. Their reactions may cause you to feel insecure, lacking in confidence or guilty about having opportunities which your parents or siblings didn't have.

But there can also be problems if everyone in the family has been to college. Can you live up to their standards? Do you have to work in the same field as them, or do they feel threatened by your choice of subject? The pressure to succeed may also contain a hidden message about not being too successful.

The most important thing with family situations of this kind is that these feelings need to be acknowledged by being talked about. This draws their sting, and makes them easier to deal with.

How will I deal with the practical issues?

Accommodation, finance, food, and travel can all present daunting problems in your first weeks.

Ask for help
Ask for help from older students, from other first-years, from your teachers. Don't be proud! You are not alone in your difficulties. There should also be institutional sources of advice and information. Most colleges should have an accommodation office, to help you find somewhere to live, and a student advisory service to give information of other kinds. There should also be a students' union. The students' union will often publish a handbook or welfare manual outlining sources of help.

Eat!
Use the canteens, if any, and if the food is bearable, especially at the beginning. It is very important to eat properly, and not to exist on snacks and beer or coffee. If you are anxious, preparing your own food may feel like too much trouble; but if you go to the canteen you will be fed, as well as having the opportunity to meet people and make friends. If there is no canteen, or the food is uneatable, join the students' union and campaign for change!

Meet people
Seek out other newcomers. Loneliness can make the challenges of your new life seem much worse. Yet when you start, everyone is alone. Colleges recognise this and often organise 'getting to know you' social events, 'freshers' fairs' and the like. Take advantage of these and any other social opportunities. At the very beginning of your first term, when you first arrive, is a key time for meeting friends. Use strategies like propping your door open if you are in a hall of residence so that you are available to get to know.

If you are shy, you may find it very difficult to join in. But it is important to remember that there will be many students who are feeling nervous and putting a brave face on it. If there is something that especially interests you, such as music or a sport, find out if there is a college society which focuses on this. Once you have found some kindred spirits, student life will seem much more manageable.

Share accommodation
Live with others to start with, if at all possible. If you can't get a place in a hall of residence or student flat, try and find a flatshare. Avoid being isolated in a bedsit where there are no other students. In this way you can not only avoid loneliness, but organise shared housework and meals.

• The above is an extract from *How to cope with the stress of student life*, published by MIND. See page 39 for address details.   © MIND

The feel-bad factor

Adolescence is often associated with conflict and universal emotional turmoil – however, there seems to be a lot more to it. Julia Derbyshire describes the findings of her study exploring the connection between stress and teenage depression.

Popular views of adolescence have portrayed it as an inevitably stressful and stormy period, full of universal emotional turmoil and conflicts. More recent research has called these assumptions into question, showing that a smooth passage through this life period is perfectly possible.

Nevertheless, evidence from North America and Britain continues to show that for many the onset of adolescence is associated with problems of mood and behaviour. More clinical disorders begin to emerge during early to mid-adolescence, along with marked sex differences, especially a higher incidence of depression and eating disorders in young women.

Research findings suggest that early adolescence may be a period of particular vulnerability to stress because a number of important changes in different life domains begin to pile up. Many young people in Britain have to cope with the biological changes of puberty as well as with the social changes involved in the transition to high school. Together, these changes have far-reaching implications for peer group relations, friendships, sexual relationships and the young person's self-concept – a build-up of stressful circumstances that may well result in poor physical or psychological health.

In the light of documented increases in rates of youth suicide and substance abuse, the potential individual and societal costs of stress in young people cannot be lightly dismissed.

For adolescents, as for adults, stressful major life events such as divorce and moving home have been shown to be associated with health problems. Possibly even more important, however, is the cumulative impact of daily hassles such as arguments, money problems and work pressures. Stressful circumstances will not necessarily result in ill health, and to some extent they provide an opportunity for growth and development, but the risk to an individual is bound up with that person's own perception of the circumstances and their ability to cope.

Research evidence from Scandinavia, North America and New Zealand shows that depression, anxiety and physical illness symptoms can all be associated with accumulated stressful circumstances in adolescents, with a peak of problems around the age of 13. In Britain, however, adolescent depression has primarily been investigated in young people referred for psychiatric help, with relatively little attention to depression among 'normal' high school pupils or to possible associations with stress-provoking circumstances.

With this in mind, our questionnaire study aimed to explore stressful life events and daily hassles, depression and physical symptoms among 11-to 14-year-olds. A checklist of physical symptoms was used alongside an established self-report measure of childhood and adolescent depression. Stressful circumstances were rated on a scale including both major events such as parental divorce and changing school, and daily hassles such as being left out, homework pressures, arguments at home, lack of money, boredom and pressure to conform.

In order to account for individual differences in the perception of stressful events, participants were required to rate each circumstance on a scale of 0–4, saying how often it had occurred and how bad it felt. After an initial pilot test with 14 young volunteers, the full study was carried out in a mixed-sex comprehensive high school in an urban industrial area of east Lancashire. Overall, 112 pupils aged 11 to 14 completed the questionnaires, which were presented within the school's personal and social education programme. Opportunity was also given for additional comment and feedback.

The results were in line with expectations and showed that a high measure of stressful life circumstances was associated with high depression and high physical symptoms scores. In addition to the total symptoms scores, feeling sick, stomach ache, headache and dizziness were each individually associated with a build-up of stressful circumstances. The most frequently reported physical symptom was headache, followed by stomach ache, aching muscles and feeling sick. Girls were found to be significantly more vulnerable than boys, although the sex difference on the depression measure was not as great as expected. There was some indication of increasing vulnerability with age.

A further finding was that a rather high 31 per cent of participants scored highly on the depression

measure, which indicated a possible clinical disorder, with a small minority of these scoring very high. This measure involves self-reporting of depressed mood and depression symptoms, such as constant tiredness, indecisiveness, loss of enjoyment and thoughts of self-harm.

School support, especially from teachers, has been shown in other studies to be very valuable

Self-reporting has limitations and some of the responses will of course reflect normal periods of sadness. Therefore, it remains arguable as to how far these high scores would predict a full clinical diagnosis of depression. Nevertheless, the results clearly show that although the case for universal adolescent emotional turmoil may have been overstated in the past, inner feelings of sadness and depression are quite common in this age group and cause considerable suffering to the individual, which unfortunately may go unnoticed by the adults around.

The measure of stressful circumstances was accepted as relevant by the participants and each of the items made at least some people 'feel bad'. Not having enough money to spend emerged as top of the four most important sources of stress identified. Conflict at home, either with or between parents, came second, although, as others have found, family support is positively related to good adjustment and close relationships with parents can help to buffer the effects of other negative events. The important subject of peer relations featured in the strong response to 'feeling left out', which came fourth. In third place was 'having nothing to do', highlighting boredom as a serious issue which may be an ongoing problem for large numbers of today's young people. A 13-year-old girl wrote: 'Life nowadays is a big downer for teenagers. We never have anywhere safe to go.'

Many of the young respondents wrote additional comments about sources of stress which were of concern to them, but didn't feature directly on the scale. These included fights with brothers and sisters or friends, problems on the school bus, large quantities of homework, and bullying or name calling. By identifying important sources of stress as perceived by young people themselves, such a measure can play an important part in raising essential adult awareness.

A great deal of time is spent during early adolescence away from family support and in the stressful high school environment. School support, especially from teachers, has been shown in other studies to be very valuable, with implications for educational achievement as well as for avoiding physical and psychological ill health.

At least two ways of improving levels of adaptation to stress are available to schools: firstly, teaching effective coping skills, problem solving approaches and social competence, and secondly, recognising and reducing sources of stress which are under school control, for example in relation to problems with particular teachers, school work or extracurricular overload.

Competence and wellbeing in young people are important for the present and future health of the nation, and awareness of adolescent stress can help families, educators, youth workers and the wider community to work together towards this aim.

• Julia Derbyshire is a teacher (BEd) and has just completed her BSc Hons in Psychology at the University of Central Lancashire in Preston. The research described in this article was undertaken under the guidance of her tutor Dr Rosalind Bramwell.

© *Young People Now*
October, 1996

Are you worried? Are you under stress?

Confidential telephone counselling for children, young people and adults

How did Careline evolve?

Careline has been in existence since 1978 and was previously run and funded by the National Children's Home (NCH) as part of their countrywide network of Carelines. Over the years NCH closed down their Carelines in order to put their finances into developing new areas of work and the Ilford Careline was closed by NCH in September 1992.

The Careline volunteers, however, were determined to keep this important service running and embarked on an initial fundraising campaign to keep the telephone lines open. A Management Committee was formed to manage the project and we are now registered as a national charity in our own right, receiving calls from all over the country. Out of the original 9 NCH Carelines we are the only Careline to remain open. Our Patron is the actor Glen Murphy (*London's Burning*).

Callers refer themselves to our service and our details are also passed to callers from other agencies which include Childline, Child Protection Teams, Domestic Violence Units, Victim Support Schemes, Relate, MIND, Samaritans, C.A.B., Brook Advisory Centres, Rape Crisis Centres, GPs, Health Visitors, Social Workers, College Advisors, Teachers and Youth Leaders.

We are regularly referred to by agony aunts who write for national newspapers and magazines and by television companies including BBC, Granada, Carlton, LWT and HTV Wales.

Why does Careline exist?

We exist because there are many people today who are isolated by loneliness, a breakdown in relationships or by a particular personal or family problem that they can't share, and sometimes people call because there is a worry or fear which they want to talk about in confidence.

People need an empathetic, non-judgmental person at the other end of the line, who is interested in them and their feelings about whatever is troubling them.

What can Careline provide?

Careline provides confidential telephone counselling for children, young people and adults.

We offer a unique service in that we can provide instant telephone counselling to any individual on any issue.

The calls we receive include family, marital and relationship problems, rape and sexual assault, child abuse, bullying, exam worries, eating disorders, HIV/AIDS and sexual health, bereavement, drug and alcohol addictions, homelessness, disability, ethnic issues, stress, depression, loneliness, anxieties and phobias.

Careline also provides a face-to-face counselling service to adults who might otherwise find counselling beyond their resources.

At Careline we have an extensive referral system covering the whole country and can offer to refer callers to a specific agency or support group in their area if required.

'To know someone "out there" cared enough to listen to me and yet not tell me what I should or shouldn't do was the turning point' (printed with permission from an ex-client).

Careline volunteers

Careline volunteers come from a wide range of backgrounds. We have a cultural mix of volunteers and as many of our callers come from different ethnic cultures, we are able to offer other spoken languages such as Hebrew, Gujrati, Punjabi, Urdu, and Hindi. Although volunteers do not need to have any professional qualifications, we do look for warm, patient, stable, clear-headed people who have an accepting, non-judgmental attitude. We also look for common-sense and a willingness to learn because training and supervision is continuous once accepted as a volunteer counsellor.

- The above is an extract from *Are you worried? Are you under stress?*, published by Careline. See page 39 for address details.

© *Careline*

CHAPTER TWO: STRESS AT WORK

Stress at work

Information from the Mental Health Foundation

Mental health and work – some facts and figures

Why you should take mental health seriously:
- Nearly 3 in every 10 employees will have a mental health problem in any one year. The great majority of these will be anxiety and depressive disorders.
- Working days lost through mental illness cost UK industry £6200m.
- In addition, statutory sick pay and invalidity benefits cost £1114m.
- Of the 517 million working days lost through sickness absence, 18% (92 million) were due to mental illness.
- Half of all days lost through mental illness were due to anxiety and stress conditions.
- Since the 1970s sickness absence due to mental illness has increased by 20%
- Taking mental health seriously can lead to a more productive workforce and a more efficient business – it makes sense to invest in mental health.

What is stress?

Stress means different things to different people, but most commonly, it refers to *both the pressures a person is under and their reaction to them.*

Stress can be beneficial and stimulating – through increasing energy, drive and productivity, performance can be enhanced. But this requires that the person's resources are sufficient to turn their response to a challenging situation into a positive one.

Stress becomes a problem when the pressures of life and work become too much for people to cope with. This can be caused by either an excess of demands, which makes them unable to cope, or an absence of stimulation and challenge. Clearly, finding a balance is vital.

Prolonged stress causes mental and physical problems. Other sections of this pack describe the warning signs, and discuss in more detail the causes, implications for work-related problems and the role of the employer.

How does stress at work manifest itself?

Many people at work will be experiencing some aspects of stress at any point in time (stress is part of our lives). Employers cannot take responsibility for it all. What they should be watching out for, however, are the signs that an individual or group of employees are so stressed that their health and/or functioning is affected. An increase in the rates of any of the following may well be a sign that something is wrong and that an employer needs to take special action:
- sickness
- poor performance
- disputes and disaffection
- poor time-keeping
- staff turnover
- grievances and complaints
- alcohol consumption.

What can give rise to stress at work?

It is unlikely that any single issue will be the cause of someone becoming stressed at work. Stress tends to build up over a period of time through a combination of circumstances, some of which may not be directly to do with the work situation at all. Difficulties in domestic relationships, money worries, even delays on the journey to work, can all build up and reduce someone's ability to cope with adverse circumstances at work. Within the work context stressful factors fall into three main groups – work content, physical conditions and work relationships. Again, there is unlikely to be a single over-riding cause but an amalgam of frustrations and worries.

Stressful work content factors can include:
- too much work
- too little work
- skills under-used
- unreasonable demands or expectations
- monotonous work with few challenges
- lack of control over how to organise work.

(Note: being under-used can be as stressful as being overworked)

Stressful physical factors can include:
- noise
- overcrowding
- excessive heat
- frequent interruptions
- always being in the public gaze
- no privacy or personal space
- a situation that feels dangerous or threatening
- not enough breaks, especially for those using machinery – VDUs etc.

Stressful work relationships can be caused by:
- lack of clear, regular support and guidance from the boss
- unclear roles, lack of clarity about responsibilities
- lack of clear priorities and targets
- inadequate feedback
- poor communication and inadequate information
- lack of opportunity to contribute.

What should employers do?

The most important thing is to accept that stress at work is an issue for employers. However, many people at work will be experiencing some aspects of stress at any point of time (stress is part of our lives) and employers cannot take responsibility for it all. What every employer should do, though, is ensure that it has taken all reasonable measures to anticipate and prevent stress arising in the first place, be able to identify problems that do arise at the earliest possible opportunity and then to support the person(s) concerned and jointly address the problems.

Employers' responsibilities concerning stress at work fall into two broad and not mutually exclusive categories:
- *Health and safety responsibilities* which mainly relate to the physical environment and to the need for specific policies and procedures.
- *Managerial responsibilities* which cover the work content and work relationships aspects.

How to address stress as a health and safety issue:
- carry out an appraisal of the physical environment
- ask all staff their views and involve them as much as possible
- agree an action plan
- consider setting up a small staff group with responsibility for monitoring environmental issues
- make sure a senior manager has formal responsibility for health and safety, including environmental stress aspects.

How to tackle stress through managerial responsibility:
- make a clear statement that your organisation recognises its responsibilities regarding stress at work and wants to develop the best possible practices for the good of all
- ensure all managers understand that they have responsibility for monitoring stress amongst their staff and for taking action to tackle it when it arises
- ensure that all managers have the necessary training to take on this responsibility
- regularly review job content (an annual review of job descriptions as a minimum)
- ensure that all staff have regular review or support meetings with their manager (monthly is usual interval) and that work load, priorities etc. are reviewed each time
- consult with staff on the development of this policy into clear procedures and the inclusion of relevant information in a staff handbook.

Stress at work is, primarily, a managerial issue. Managers can usually deal with any problems that arise providing they respond quickly and properly and gain the confidence and co-operation of the person concerned

Further action:
- build a stress education programme into your ongoing training programme to increase the ability of your employees to cope with stress. Do not, however, then take this as an opportunity to avoid doing other things to reduce stress wherever possible
- if you have not been able to deal with the problems in the way suggested above, or very stressful circumstances are inevitable in your field, consider providing your staff with access to a confidential counselling service.

Stress at work can be successfully tackled and it is in everyone's best interests to do so as soon as problems emerge.

Introduction to The Mental Health Foundation

The Mental Health Foundation is the only charity in the UK concerned with all aspects of mental health, including mental illness and learning disabilities (mental handicap).

We are dedicated to:
- supporting innovation
- increasing knowledge and awareness
- promoting change.

We do this through funding both community initiatives and research, producing training programmes and publications.

Our grants are made on the advice of specialist committees, the members of which give their time at no cost to the Foundation.

There are currently over one hundred projects which the Foundation is supporting throughout the UK. We are, however, dependent upon voluntary donations to carry out these activities; we rely on individuals, companies and trusts to support our work and provide us with the funds which are so essential to progress.

• The above is an extract from *Stress at Work*, published by the Mental Health Foundation. See page 39 for address details.

© *The Mental Health Foundation*

Stress in the workplace

Does it concern you? Report by Michiel Kompier and Lennart Levi

Do you know this man?

John, 36, married and a father of two children, works in a small factory, at an assembly line. In traditional occupational environment terms, it is a good place to work. The noise created by the machinery has been reduced to an acceptable level. Illumination is good. Temperature, flow, and humidity of the air have been adjusted to norms. John is seated in a comfortable chair, and his working posture has been adjusted to avoid unnecessary loads and twists. The risk of occupational accidents is low.

In spite of all this, John feels sad, anxious, and indeed, ill. He smokes, drinks, and eats too much. He has difficulties falling asleep in the evening, and wakes up early, feeling tired and frustrated. His wife worries about his recurrent headaches, chronic indigestion, and increase in blood pressure, as diagnosed by their family doctor. She is appalled every time he states that 'life is not worth living anymore'.

How has all this come about? Let's take a closer – and broader – look.

Facing considerable economic difficulties, John's employer has laid off some 30% of his staff, streamlining the production process, and urging all workers to 'work harder', and if necessary, longer hours. The work itself has remained highly monotonous, with a small number of simple tasks being repeated again, and again, and again.

The recent lay-offs have caused uneasiness among the workers, with mutual suspicion, hostility, and reluctance to help one another. Everyone is afraid of being next in line for lay-off. In this highly competitive setting, and with performance paid by individual piece wages, fewer and fewer are prepared

Information from the European Foundation for the Improvement of Living and Working Conditions

to lend a helping hand to their fellow workers.

This sums up a situation characterised by high demands in quantitative terms (too much to do), combined with low decision latitude (possibilities to decide what is to be done, and how), and low social support from fellow workers, together with insecurity about the future.

This combination spells 'stress', and, consequently, an increased risk of physical and mental ill health, causing suffering, absenteeism, decreased productivity, and losses, to employees and employers alike.

Do you recognise John? Is he one of your fellow workers? A member of your family? Your spouse? Or does the description fit you, give or take a few details?

If so, this should not surprise you. John's case is in no way an extreme one. His situation is part of everyday life for a considerable proportion of workers and salaried employees in countless small and medium-sized enterprises in Europe, and elsewhere. Our key questions are: (1) why is this so; and (2) can we – and you, the reader – do something to improve the situation, i.e. to reduce your stress at work, and its harmful effects on your health and wellbeing, on productivity, and on the future of your work?

What is stress?

In engineering, stress is 'a force which deforms bodies'. In medicine, the term refers to the body's strategy for adapting to whatever influences, changes, demands, and strains it

encounters. This strategy swings into action if you are assaulted on the street or insulted by your boss, expected to achieve something when you doubt that you can, or when, with or without cause, you worry about your job. You need a certain amount of responsibility, but your job offers less, or demands more. You need a certain amount of work, but you often get too much, or you are threatened with and actually get none at all – unemployment. Thus, one cause of stress at work is an inadequate fit between your work and you.

Another cause lies in *role conflicts*. We all play several roles. In our private life, we are husbands or wives; we are parents to our children, we are children to our parents; we are brothers or sisters, friends, and neighbours. At work, we are bosses, peers and subordinates. All at the same time. And the ingredients of conflicts are easy to find in trying to fill these multiple roles.

There is something common to all these cases in the way your body attempts to adapt. This common denominator – a kind of 'revving up' or 'stepping on the gas' – is stress. Your sense of control over what is happening to you is critical. When you feel in control, stress becomes the spice of life, a challenge instead of a threat. When you lack this crucial sense of control, stress can spell crisis – bad news for you, your health and your enterprise.

Stress at work

Briefly, then, stress is caused by a bad fit between you and your work, by conflicts between your roles at work and outside it, and by not having a reasonable degree of control over your own work and your own life. Thus, stress at work is caused by a multitude of demands and exposures. Some common ones include:

- Inadequate time to complete your job to your own and others' satisfaction.
- Lack of clear job description, or chain of command.
- No recognition, or reward, for good job performance.
- No opportunity to voice complaints.
- Lots of responsibilities, but little authority or decision-making capacity.
- Uncooperative or unsupportive superiors, co-workers, or subordinates.
- No control, or pride, over the finished product of your work.
- Job insecurity, no permanence of position.
- Exposure to prejudice regarding your age, gender, race, ethnicity, or religion.
- Unpleasant or hazardous physical work conditions.
- No opportunity to utilise your personal talents or abilities effectively.
- Chances for a small error or momentary lapse of attention to have serious or even disastrous consequences.

If you feel this to be part of your everyday work, it affects the rate at which processes of wear and tear in your body take place. The more 'gas' given, the higher the 'revolutions per minute' (RPMs) at which your body's engine is driven, the more rapidly your 'engine' wears out.

Stress reactions

When we are exposed to these or related stressors, most of us experience anxiety, depression, uneasiness, restlessness, or fatigue.

Stress at work can also make some of us start smoking more, or over-eating, seeking comfort in alcohol or taking unnecessary risks at work or in traffic. Many of these reactions lead to disease and premature death. Suicide is one of many examples.

Your sense of control over what is happening to you is critical. When you feel in control, stress becomes the spice of life, a challenge instead of a threat

---

We also react physiologically, with our internal organs. When you feel unjustly criticised by your supervisor, your blood pressure may increase; you may experience increased or irregular heart rate, or muscular tension with subsequent pain in the neck, head, and shoulders, or dryness of your throat and mouth, or heartburn because of over-production of acid gastric juice.

All of these stress reactions can make you suffer, become ill, and even die – through diseases of the heart and blood vessels, or cancer (from smoking too much, or eating too much fat food and too little nutritional fibre).

What can you do?

Should you see these causes and consequences as 'God-made', as a stroke of fate, and impossible to influence? Does it follow that unhealthy conditions of work should be accepted, tolerated, adapted to and possibly compensated by higher pay? Or should such conditions be improved, wherever possible, and their consequences – in terms of occupational stress and disease – ameliorated, or even prevented? And, last but not least, should not conditions which promote health, wellbeing, and productivity at work be promoted?

To accomplish this, you need to identify stressors, stress reactions, and stress-related ill health at your job. There are several reasons for doing this: stress is a problem both for you, the worker, and your company; work stress problems are on the increase; it is a legal obligation according to the E.U. Framework Directive on Health and Safety; and many of the stressors and consequences are avoidable and can be adjusted by you and your employer acting together in your own and your mutual interests.

- The above is an extract from *Stress at work – Does it concern you?*, published by the European Foundation for the Improvement of Living and Working Conditions. See page 39 for address details.

© *European Foundation for the Improvement of Living and Working Conditions*

How stress at work could be shrinking your brain

By Daniel Jeffreys

When life becomes too stressful, your head aches and you feel like screaming. When the pain becomes too extreme, it can feel as if the stress headache is making your brain shrink.

Stress is the deadly side-effect of busy lives. Many doctors say stress-related death has now reached epidemic proportions.

When a young person keels over from stress, it is usually the heart that has been damaged, but a dramatic new study shows that the brain may be just as much at risk.

Severe stress may cause vital parts of the brain's tissue to shrivel. The result can be a loss of short-term memory, an inability to concentrate and mental instability.

That feeling of a brain that's shrinking is a reality and it's caused by a chemical our bodies must produce for us to function.

These startling conclusions come from a study co-ordinated by Dr Robert Sapolsky at California's Stanford University.

He has studied stress in animals for two decades by tracking the effects of cortisol, a chemical that floods the brain along with adrenaline at times of severe stress.

He found that repeated doses of cortisol can damage certain control centres in the brain, especially those dealing with memory. His findings are published in the latest edition of *Science*, the monthly US journal.

'Cortisol is the main chemical the body uses to arouse itself when danger threatens,' he says.

'It triggers an increase in blood pressure and mobilises energy from fat tissue and the liver.

'The dark side of this picture is the effects on the brain. Cortisol is necessary for survival, but it can be disastrous to the brain if it is secreted for months on end.

'We've known that it could lead to hypertension or diabetes. Now we are finding it also damages the brain.'

> **The most surprising aspect of this new research is that the body is designed to self-destruct in the face of too much stress**

Anyone who lives with severe stress on a daily basis is at risk. The most dangerous professions are the Armed Services, firemen, police officers, ambulancemen, surgeons and foreign exchange traders.

People who are in stressful relationships with constant arguments or abuse are also vulnerable to brain damage. But anybody who feels life is excessively stressful or suffers from panic attacks is at risk.

The brain needs a certain amount of cortisol to perform its normal tasks. The hormone is released by the tiny, triangular adrenal glands on top of the kidneys. They are forced to excrete cortisol in excessive amounts in response to ageing, alcohol and stress.

Dr Sapolsky's research shows that a combination of stress and alcohol is likely to speed up brain damage.

'This is really a mechanism by which the body attacks its own brain,' he says. 'We can't live without these chemicals but if they spill around too freely they become corrosive, just like battery acid spilt on the other parts of a car's engine.'

The most surprising aspect of this new research is that the body is designed to self-destruct in the face of too much stress.

'Severe trauma produces profound and long-lasting changes in brain function,' says Dr Dennis Chaney, an American psychiatrist who worked with Dr Sapolsky.

'The idea that severe stress or trauma can damage the brain is remarkable. Yet we have seen enough examples to show that we may be killing our minds with stress.

'We need to re-think how we deal with stress and the way we expose people to stressful situations.'

Dr Chaney's studies of Vietnam veterans show that those who suffer stress symptoms such as repetitive nightmares or flashbacks have an 8 per cent reduction in the size of their hippocampus – part of the lateral ventricle of the brain – compared to other people.

The veterans performed badly in memory tests with scores 40 per cent below average.

There is a hippocampus on the left and right sides of the brain. It is shaped like a sea horse and plays a vital role in memory as it holds new information for a few seconds before it is forgotten or processed into long-term memory. Another recent study of Vietnam veterans by New York psychiatrist Dr Roger Pitman found that soldiers who had been in the most extreme forms of combat have a 25 to 30 per cent shrinkage in their hippocampus.

The research seems to prove a frightening proposition – place people under traumatic stress repeatedly and their brains shrivel up.

Dr Sapolsky's work with cortisol also indicates that stress may play a part in infertility. And adults who were victims of repeated sexual assault or abuse as children are also likely to have memory damage.

Connecticut neuroscientist Dr Douglas Bremner has discovered that the hippocampus of more than 100 victims of childhood abuse was 10 per cent smaller than average and the patients had damaged short-term memories.

A simple test can show if your memory has been affected by stress. Get somebody to tell you a simple story. Repeat it to them immediately. Then do the same thing 15 minutes later.

People with a damaged hippocampus usually get 40 pc of the story wrong the second time they re-tell the story.

Even people who suffer just slightly above-average levels of stress may be at risk from brain damage.

'Some people have brains that are hypersensitive to cortisol,' says Dr Rachel Yehuda, a New York psychologist who worked on Dr Sapolsky's research programme.

'This can develop over time. People who are repeatedly exposed to stress seem to reset the levels of cortisol required to help them deal with the external threat.

'If they suddenly release higher levels, the brain may be damaged.'

Doctors do not know if the effects of stress on the brain are reversible or if stress chemicals can be blocked by other drugs.

Dr Sapolsky and Dr Chaney are working on further research to answer these questions. Next month, they will begin taking brain scans of police officers, firefighters and inner-city children.

'We are under increasing amounts of stress as our world becomes more complex,' says Dr Sapolsky.

'Many of the effects of stress on the brain are still unknown. In ten or 20 years, stress damage to the brain may be killing more people than heart disease unless we can find ways of minimising the damage.'

© *The Daily Mail*
August, 1996

Managing stress

Issue No 18 of *Managing Best Practice* reports on stress. Below is a digest of the report's survey of 699 managers.

Key survey findings

- An overwhelming 83% of managers said that stress is a problem in their organisations.
- The main organisational effects of stress are increased absenteeism, decreased productivity, poor judgement, quality and customer care.
- Nearly half of those who responded said that stress had been a cost for their organisations over the last two years. A similar proportion had no idea whether stress was a cost or not.
- Over the last three years, awareness of the issue of stress has increased in three-quarters of the organisations surveyed. A similar proportion said that actual levels of stress had increased.
- Stress is most commonly seen by organisations as an integral part of many jobs; a symptom of organisational change; an indication of overwork; or an illness. Only 7% of managers said that it was regarded as an excuse for time off.
- The average line manager would be sympathetic if a member of their team said they were suffering from stress, but over a third of respondents said that managers would do nothing in response.
- The most common causes of stress are life events (such as divorce); an increased workload due to downsizing; job insecurity; rapid change; long working hours; and difficulty balancing home and work.
- The key symptoms of stress are increased absence, irritability, permanent fatigue, emotional behaviour and mistakes.
- Stress is experienced by all groups of employees, though middle managers experience the most. Men experience stress more often than women, and the older employees are, the more likely they are to experience stress on a regular basis.
- A third of organisations have taken action to help employees cope with general stress, while only a fifth have introduced measures to help prevent work-related stress.
- The most effective method of reducing stress is maintaining good employee communications. Stress awareness training for managers and employees and the promotion of wellbeing are also effective.
- Supportive managers and colleagues are the most effective factors in helping employees cope with stress, followed by stress awareness training and counselling/support services.

- The above is an extract from *Managing Best Practice*, published by The Industrial Society. See page 39 for address details.

© *The Industrial Society*

Are managers under stress?

A survey of management morale

Introduction

The Institute of Management (IM), supported by health products manufacturer Lanes, has undertaken major new research into stress management issues. The findings are presented in full in an IM research report and are summarised here.

The objective of the research project was to explore the impact of job-related stress among managers and how far certain aspects may have changed since 1993 when previous IM research into stress was carried out. What are the workplace and lifestyle factors which contribute to stress and how can these be tackled? The IM survey therefore sought to investigate the extent and impact of organisational changes: changing work patterns: attitudes and beliefs about stress: sources of stress outside of work: stress symptoms experienced and remedies used to treat them.

Research for the project was conducted in January 1996, when the views of nearly 1,100 managers were obtained from a postal questionnaire sent to a random sample of 3,000 individual IM members. This represents a response rate of 36 per cent.

Background

Some individuals, in the short term, appear to cope with the pressures which accompany responsibility and which are part of the daily routine. These often have a positive effect on motivation and job satisfaction; it is only when individual thresholds are broken that the problems of stress occur. The detrimental effects of poorly managed stress on the organisation show in terms of inefficiency, reduced productivity and absenteeism. An estimated 270,000 people take time off work every day because of work-related stress: this represents a cumulative cost in terms of sick pay, lost production and NHS charges of around £7 billion annually.

Away from the organisational environment, troubles often start when too many life events occur at once as these can overtax an individual's ability to cope. Life events such as the death of someone close, divorce, serious illness, a large mortgage and even happy occasions such as holiday or marriage can all be stressful. Some of these events such as death or illness are unpredictable, while others are brought on by choice. Successful stress management therefore involves not creating unnecessary change in potentially turbulent times.

Key findings

Stress at work

- Organisational changes such as redundancies, introduction of new technology and loss of key personnel place extra demands on managers and increase stress. More than eight in ten managers reported that their workload had increased over the past year, of which 47 per cent felt it had increased greatly.
- Unpaid overtime hours are widespread. Nearly six in ten respondents claim that they always work in excess of their official working week, while one in seven always work at weekends.
- Unreasonable deadlines and office politics were identified as the two most stressful work issues by about half of respondents. Thirty per cent of women had suffered stress due to bullying or intimidating behaviour.
- It is concerning that 65 per cent of managers do not agree that their professional and personal lives are in balance, while only half of respondents to the 1996 survey agree that they look forward to going to work.
- Seventy per cent of organisations offer their staff neither stress counselling nor an Employee Assistance Programme.

Lifestyle stress

- Financial pressures caused concern for over half of the sample, while negative equity affected 15 per cent. Over a third agreed that the journey to work/commuting was a source of stress; Christmas and going on holiday were stressful for about a third and a quarter of respondents respectively.
- Forty per cent of male respondents feel they do not spend enough time with their children and cited this a source of stress. Over half of female respondents find arranging household/ domestic matters a

source of stress and a quarter found arranging childcare a problem.
- Self-employed respondents were more likely to agree that they had a good balance between home and work; that they were fully in control of their job and could cope with stress.

Impact of stress
- Five per cent of respondents strongly agreed that they needed help in dealing with stress, although 65 per cent claim they can cope with their current stress levels. Middle and junior managers however were less likely to agree.
- Symptoms of stress such as tiredness, irritability and disturbed sleep were experienced by over 80 per cent of respondents.
- Physical activity/exercise was seen as an effective antidote to stress by seven in ten respondents, while alternative/complementary stress remedies are likely to become more popular in future. Women were more likely than men to have tried aromatherapy, reflexology or yoga to relieve stress.
- The impact of stress on work and home life is obviously far-reaching and has increased over the past three years. The percentage of respondents who believe that stress has a minimal impact on five aspects of their lives has virtually halved since the previous survey.

Conclusions

While the pace of change and restructuring continues, organisations seem to have failed in reassessing the nature and priority of managerial work. Redundancies, introduction of new technology and loss of key personnel have been experienced by almost half of respondents in the past year. This has resulted in fewer managers doing more, facing heavier workloads and suffering increased stress.

The major causes of stress in the workplace are unreasonable deadlines and office politics. Flatter management structures do not however lead to the anticipated advances in communications, efficiency, decision-making and employee involvement.

This research confirms that stress affects all levels and types of manager. Almost 90 per cent of respondents believe that stress is having an adverse effect on morale, health, work effectiveness and relationships.

The correct balance is not always easy to find either between commitment to work and the stress it generates, or between work and family. Women managers continue to have to juggle domestic and professional responsibilities, while men want to spend more time with their children and both sexes suffer stress accordingly.

Stress tolerance and the ability to work under pressure are often cited as pre-requisites in job advertisements. It is now time for the business community to abandon the macho and heroic image of stress and encourage greater co-operation and support.

The Institute of Management represents around 73,000 individual managers, making it the largest broadly based management institute in the UK. It also embraces 700 subscribing organisations representing around 3 million employees.

The IM is the driving force behind the development and exercise of professional management and combines management theory and practice in its extensive portfolio of management services. These are designed to help managers at all levels and in all disciplines to develop their full potential. They include the IM's nationally recognised management development qualifications and a pre-eminent information service.

G.R. Lane Health Products Limited, established over 60 years ago, manufactures a wide range of herbal remedies, vitamin and mineral supplements, health foods and natural cosmetics.

- *Are Managers Under Stress?, a survey of management morale*, is an IM research report by Karen Charlesworth. Price: £25 to IM members and £50 to non-members.
Available from: The Representation Unit, The Institute of Management, 2 Savoy Court Strand, London WC2R 0EZ

© *The Institute of Management September, 1996*

Why stress is breeding the office superbully

By Tony Hazell

An Institute of Personnel and Development survey was conducted by Harris Research, who interviewed more than 1,000 people.

Just over half of those who have been bullied say it is common in their organisation, and a quarter say it has got worse in the past year.

But some experts warn that weak staff often fail to see the difference between strong management and bullying. A quarter agreed with the statement that: 'It's only over-sensitive people who complain about bullying – most people just accept it as a fact of working life.'

The focus of the report is not about one-off incidents where the boss explodes in frustration. They are where someone has been persistently offensive or abusive and used intimidating or insulting behaviour, leaving the bullied person feeling upset, threatened, humiliated and vulnerable. Most are a deliberate attempt to undermine self-confidence and many involve an abuse of power.

Bullying is not confined to the lower ranks, nor is it always boss bullying subordinate. Nearly a quarter of middle managers and one in five professionals say their boss has bullied them.

More insidious bullying, such as constant undervaluation of efforts or excessive criticism, is also widespread. Physical assault was reported by one in 12 victims.

Some bullying takes place in team cultures – for example, in sales departments – where pressure is put on the weakest member of the team.

Melissa Compton Edwards, who co-ordinated the research for the IPD, says that the pressure felt by executives to meet performance targets could push them into bullying their direct subordinates into delivering the impossible. 'Macho management styles can result in demoralisation, poor performance and stress-related absenteeism,' she says. Most victims felt that the bully could not cope with his or her own job, or was motivated by jealousy.

> *'At least once a week I was called into his office and dressed down for the tiniest things. It got so that I dreaded going to work'*

But bullying is complex, says psychotherapist Neil Crawford, a consultant at London's Tavistock Clinic.

Some victims collude with the aggressor rather than risk the fight escalating. Others may even provoke bullies.

'Some people do not understand that their actions can upset others,' says Mr Crawford. 'They almost irritate people into bullying them without realising it.'

The suggestion that some people have a personality that attracts bullies gets some backing from the report. A third of those who were bullied at work had also been bullied as a child.

Most people said that bullying can never be justified, but Mr Crawford warns that some bosses thrive on conflict. He says: 'If you fight these psychopathic managers, they may regard it as a challenge and attempt to destroy you at all costs.'

With them, the only answer could be to find another job.

Simon's story

Bullying can happen at all levels and in all kinds of organisations.

Simon, 37, suffered for two years at the hands of a bully before he quit his job at a business in Glasgow. Having joined at a junior level, he worked his way up to a management position within four years. 'I always got above-average pay rises and bonuses,' he says. 'I enjoyed my work. I was successful and rising in the firm and could have happily stayed there for the rest of my working life.'

Then, after ten years working within the company, things changed. His boss was made redundant during the recession and, after a few months, a new, heavy-handed manager was appointed.

'At least once a week I was called into his office and dressed down for the tiniest things. It got so that I dreaded going to work.

'My work suffered. I became slower and nervous, which led me to make errors.'

His personal life and health also suffered. 'I was waking at night with chest pains, which my doctor said were anxiety attacks. He sent me to a counsellor. My relationship with my wife and child also came under strain.'

Eventually, Simon resigned to take another job. 'I felt I had no choice. It concerns me that companies can lose dedicated, conscientious workers because of one person,' he says.

Since Simon resigned two years ago, the manager he worked under has been dismissed for unrelated events.

© The Daily Mail November, 1996

Workplace bullying may cost employers and state £12 billion a year

Following a survey on workplace bullying by the Institute of Personnel and Development (IPD) last Thursday (28/11/96) comes a ground-breaking book by Tim Field. *Bully in sight: how to predict, resist, challenge and combat workplace bullying*, with a foreword by Diana Lamplugh OBE, reveals a catalogue of abuse, mostly in the guise of 'management'.

The book imparts detailed insight into how, why, when and where bullies bully, the most serious types of bullying, and the circumstances that give rise to and sustain bullying. A wealth of suggestions and ideas for standing up and fighting back are also offered.

Much of this insight into bullying is appearing in print for the first time, the author believes. Detailed descriptions of how to recognise both the appalling psychiatric injuries *and* the causes are likely to set alarm bells ringing in employers' legal departments, especially with the predictable and foreseeable nature of bullying explained.

'Even the IPD's figure of 1 in 8 people reporting being bullied at work in the last five years may be conservative,' comments Tim Field. 'Bullying is an abuse which often goes on behind closed doors with no witnesses; a similar study in 1994 by Staffordshire University Business School showed that in a survey of 1137 employees, one in two said they were being or had been bullied at some time in their working life. The presence of the IPD survey says more than the content,' adds Tim. 'For such a respected professional body as the IPD to acknowledge publicly that bullying is a problem could be the turning point and the culmination of nearly a decade of work initiated by the late Andrea Adams.'

With potentially between 2.5 and 10 million employees affected, the costs are staggering. In 1994, the Health & Safety Executive (HSE) estimated the cost of stress and stress-related illness to be in the order of £4 billion. Unofficial estimates put the cost as high as £12 billion or more. The author believes that bullying is one of the main causes of stress – perhaps *the* main cause of stress today. 'After last week's budget, the Chancellor would do well to note that this cost represents something like 2p on the basic rate of income tax,' observes Tim.

> **The most common type of caller is female, 45–50ish, professional or office-based**

Since 1 January 1996 Tim has been running a national Workplace Bullying Advice Line from his home in South Oxfordshire. In under twelve months he has taken over 500 calls, of which more than 470 are cases of bullying.

'Many callers are in tears, often approaching mental breakdown, some are in breakdown as they talk to me,' reports Tim. 'At least 10% of callers admit to having considered suicide, some have already attempted it and a couple of cases involve actual suicide. The true figure is probably much higher.'

Calls come from all sectors of the workplace (including the voluntary sector); the most common type of caller is female, 45–50ish, professional or office-based. The next most common are males 45–55ish, professional or office-based.

Now an author, trainer and independent consultant, Tim liaises with many organisations in the field of workplace bullying, including the Andrea Adams Trust, the Campaign Against Bullying At Work (CABAW), and The Suzy Lamplugh Trust.

- The above is an extract from a press release regarding Tim Field's book, *Bully in sight: how to predict, resist, challenge and combat workplace bullying*, available from Workplace Bullying. See page 39 for address details.

© *Tim Field*

The cost of stress

Who suffers from stress?

Most of us can cope with and, indeed, may need a certain amount of pressure in our lives. However, research shows that stress can be damaging to people in situations where demands exceed resources for coping, where there is little control over what is happening and where there is a lack of social and emotional support. Stress without relief can result in a downward spiral into depression. There is a well-known link between depression and suicide.[1]

Figures on deaths by suicide show that some occupational groups are at higher risk of suicide than others, for a variety of reasons including stress.

There has been much publicity recently about those in the healthcare and agricultural professions suffering unusually high levels of stress. This is, unfortunately, borne out in the statistics. Male and female doctors, female nurses, farmers and farmer's wives all show higher rates of suicide than others of their age and sex. Female doctors are at over three times the risk of the average woman of working age, and nurses account for 5% of all female suicides.

The cost of stress

Stress may be work-related or result from personal causes; often it is impossible to separate the two. The costs can be measured in many different ways but the results have an impact on individuals and organisations in the forms of inefficiency, higher accident rates, sickness absence, early retirement on medical grounds and even premature death.

A survey of self-reported work-related illness in 1990[3] found that stress and depression was the second most common cause of sickness absence after musculoskeletal health problems such as backache. The highest rate of stress was found to be in men of 45–64 years of age. This survey found that 1.7 million working days were lost to work-related stress and depression alone.[4]

Various experts have made estimates of the costs – a survey by MIND suggested that between 25 and 50% of all sickness absence was attributable to stress, at a cost of £7 billion per year in the UK.[5] However, the full price is currently impossible to quantify.

The CBI estimates the cost at £3.7 billion with 91 million days lost as a result of 'mental ill health'. A survey of CBI members estimated that a third of all sick leave was related to effects of stress, anxiety and depression.[6]

Whatever the true costs, they are high and taxing to business when the need both to control costs and to ensure an effective and healthy workforce is greater than ever.

Case studies

Marks & Spencer Occupational Health Services and Welfare Services

Health Services promotes and maintains the physical, psychological and social well-being of staff. A team of occupational health physicians and advisors works with Marks & Spencer staff to provide help and information on a wide variety of medical issues.

They also run extensive screening programmes and pioneer new services to meet the needs of their staff.

High-risk occupational groups in England and Wales[2]

Occupation	PMR – suicide risk (%)	Number of suicides 1988-92
Men aged 16–64		
Vets	361	18
Pharmacists	199	18
Dental practitioners	194	18
Chemical scientists / Engineers	156	38
Forestry workers	155	27
University academic staff	152	27
Farmers	145	177
Medical practitioners	144	60
Women aged 16–59		
Ambulance women	402	3
Vets	387	3
Government inspectors	365	3
Medical practitioners	322	25
Nurses	154	247
Pharmacists	141	4
Literary / Artistic professions	112	42

PMR is Proportional Mortality Ratio, a measure of suicide risk. The average for men aged 16–64 and women aged 16–59 = 100. Thus a PMR of 365 for female government inspectors indicates that this group is at 3.65 times the risk of suicide as the average woman aged between 16 and 59.

Welfare Services offers a specialist support service for current and retired employees considering their social and welfare needs, the changing commercial environment and personal priorities.

The department runs a Welfare Helpline for all employees and retired staff, and has developed a programme of courses called Planning for the Future, which help staff to make decisions for the future in areas of finance and welfare.

The following two case studies illustrate how individuals can be helped to manage stressful situations in the work environment.

Case study 1

A senior manager who was perceived as being highly successful in his role was offered a job change to a higher level in a different category of employment. Unfortunately he rapidly failed in his new appointment, his personal performance as well as his work performance was seen to suffer. As soon as there was a recognition that this was resulting in a stress reaction, he was referred to the Occupational Health Service. He took three months' sick leave during which he received psychological counselling and was gradually rehabilitated to his originally challenging role at pre-promotion level. Now he has regained his health and continues to be a valuable employee.

Case study 2

A young woman self-referred to the Occupational Health Service with a minor medical problem. On closer questioning it was found to be related to the fact that her parents were separated. In the preceding two months she had taken a considerable amount of sick leave because of minor medical problems and was genuinely concerned that her health was deteriorating. The physician who spoke to her explored the fact that both parents were using her as a sounding board and that she was finding the conflict difficult to resolve. As a result of the counselling she received she developed more insight and has been well since. She has not lost a day through ill health in the year that has followed her counselling.

References

1. Department of Health (NHS Health Advisory Service), (1994) 'Suicide Prevention: The Challenge Confronted. A manual of guidance for the purchasers and providers of Mental Health Care', HMSO, London
2. Kelly, S Charlton, J and Jenkins, R (1995) 'Suicide deaths in England and Wales, 1982–92: the contribution of occupation and geography'. Population Trends, 80
3. Hodgson, JT, Jones, JR, Elliott RC and Osman, R (1993) 'Self-reported work-related illness. Results from a trailer questionnaire on the 1990 Labour Force Survey in England and Wales', Research Paper 33, HSE Books, Sudbury
4. Davies, NV and Teasdale, P (1994) 'The costs to the British economy of work accidents and work-related ill health', HSE Books, Sudbury
5. MIND (1992) 'The MIND Survey: Stress at Work', MIND, London
6. Reported in: Department of Health (1995) 'ABC of Health Promotion in the Workplace', Health Information Service, 0800 665544

• The above is an extract from *The cost of stress*, published by The Samaritans. See page 39 for address details.
© *The Samaritans*

The legal position

There is no specific legislation on controlling stress at work. Not enough is known to set detailed standards or requirements. However,

- employers have a duty under the Health and Safety at Work Act 1974 to ensure, so far as is reasonably practicable, that their workplaces are safe and healthy;

- under the Management of Health and Safety Regulations 1993 employers are obliged to assess the nature and scale of risks to health in their workplace and base their control measures on it.

Ill health resulting from stress caused at work has to be treated the same as ill health due to other, physical causes present in the workplace. This means that employers do have a legal duty to take reasonable care to ensure that health is not placed at risk through excessive and sustained levels of stress arising from the way work is organised, the way people deal with each other at their work or from the day-to-day demands placed on their workforce. Employers should bear stress in mind when assessing possible health hazards in their workplaces, keeping an eye out for developing problems and being prepared to act if harm to health seems likely. In other words, stress should be treated like any other health hazard.

Employers are not under a legal duty to prevent ill health due to stress arising from circumstances outside work, such as personal or domestic problems. But it may be in their own as well as their employees' interests to deal sympathetically with staff whose domestic circumstances or state of health make it difficult for them to cope for the time being with the pressures of work.

• The above is an extract from *Stress at Work – A guide for employers* published by the Health and Safety Executive. Ref. HS (G) 116, ISBN 0 7176 0733 X. Copies are available, price £5.25, from HSE Books, PO Box 1999, Sudbury, Suffolk CO10 6FS (tel 01787 881165 or fax 01787 313995) or through good booksellers.
© *Health and Safety Executive*

CHAPTER THREE: COPING WITH STRESS

What makes you angry?

Rage stories are never far from the headlines – but why are we all so angry? We found out . . .

By Julie Fairhead and Martin Daubney

A few years ago the term didn't exist. Now, it seems, we can't turn on the TV or open a newspaper without hearing about another rage attack.

Whether it's trolley rage, queue rage, cinema rage, golf rage, pedestrian rage or, of course, road rage, there's no doubt that as a phenomenon, those sudden outbreaks of anger are becoming the norm. We seem to be turning into an angry nation. Or are we?

To find out, we polled 1,000 women and men for their views; nearly 90 per cent of those surveyed think we're now far angrier than we were just 10 years ago.

And they are talking from experience. As many as half of those surveyed have actually been on the receiving end of somebody else's rage. While over a quarter have totally lost control of their temper – with potentially explosive consequences.

Michelle and Andrew Powell know what it's like to be in the firing line.

> **To find out, we polled 1,000 women and men for their views; nearly 90 per cent of those surveyed think we're now far angrier than we were just 10 years ago**

As Andrew pulled their Skoda car up at the lights near their home in Hove, Sussex, in August 1995, another car suddenly cut sharply in front of them, causing them to brake hard. 'Stupid idiot,' muttered Andrew, 32.

Before Andrew could blink, the male driver and his girl passenger had flung open their doors and begun marching towards them.

'I stepped out of our car to see what they wanted and the girl grabbed my hair and began kicking and punching me,' recalls beauty therapist Michelle, 32.

'She was like a pit bull terrier. I didn't know what we'd done to prompt such anger.'

But worse was to come. Remembers Andrew: 'I asked the man to help me break it up, but instead, he went back to his car and

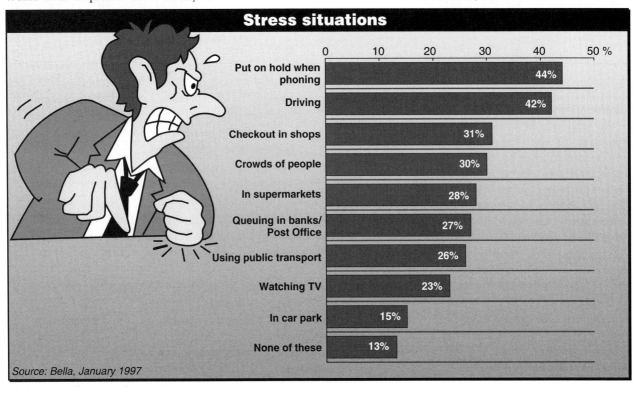

Stress situations

Situation	%
Put on hold when phoning	44%
Driving	42%
Checkout in shops	31%
Crowds of people	30%
In supermarkets	28%
Queuing in banks/Post Office	27%
Using public transport	26%
Watching TV	23%
In car park	15%
None of these	13%

Source: Bella, January 1997

got a rounders bat! He hit me on the head and I collapsed.'

Michelle, who was covered in scratches and bruises, continues: 'One minute we'd been going shopping, the next Andrew was slumped over our car and there was blood everywhere.'

Witnesses took the attackers' registration as they sped away and called the police.

Last September, at Lewes Crown Court, Christopher Holmes, 21, was convicted of causing grievous bodily harm and jailed for four years. His girlfriend, Elizabeth Holding, 20, was charged with actual bodily harm and jailed for six months. The attack has left the couple bemused.

'He must have read my lips in his mirror as I complained about his driving,' says Andrew. 'I wasn't very polite, but that was no reason to go for us the way they did.

'We couldn't believe that something so apparently trivial ended in such violence.'

Although driving is guaranteed to make many people lose their temper, it's certainly not the only stressful situation responsible for anger outbursts, as our chart shows.

And surprisingly, women are *more* likely to lose their tempers in seven out of those 10 scenarios.

So, what kinds of people suffer from rage? Well, it seems very few of us are totally calm. The younger people are, the more likely they are to fly off the handle. Over a third of 18–24 year-olds have difficulty controlling their temper. Mums and dads also have shorter tempers than those without kids.

Younger people are most likely to be the victims of rage attacks, with nearly two-thirds complaining of being attacked.

A respectable lawyer was the last person temp secretary Irene Young expected to burst into a violent rage. But that's exactly what happened within hours of her going to work at John Macleod's solicitors firm in November 1994.

Irene, 35, from Bradford, hadn't had enough time to make an important personal call before leaving for work that day, so she decided to use the company phone during her lunch break.

Seeing red?
How to deal with rage

- Don't be provoked into fighting or shouting back in a 'rage' situation. It will achieve nothing expect to further fuel the anger of those around you. You never know how strangers will react.

- Remember: it takes a better person to walk away than to stand and slug it out.

- Take deep breaths and listen to what your internal voices are saying, then calm yourself down.

- Think positive thoughts, for example, about a pleasant holiday or your loved ones.

- There are now a number of anger management courses available. Contact your GP for details.

- If you're the victim of road rage, stay in your vehicle, lock your doors, avoid eye contact and if possible, drive safely and calmly away.

Poll by NOP Consumer Market Research

Younger people are most likely to be the victims of rage attacks, with nearly two-thirds complaining of being attacked

But at that moment her boss John Macleod came out of his office – and the 16-stone lawyer went berserk.

Says Irene: 'He called me a slag and said he wasn't paying me for the two hours' work I'd done.

'He grabbed me by the hair and shoved me forcefully out of the door.

'His face was bright red with anger. I was absolutely terrified.'

In June 1995, Irene took Macleod to an industrial tribunal and received £8,300 for sex discrimination.

He admitted insulting Irene and getting her in a bear hug but he said he was angry because her call amounted to 'taking office property without permission'.

'I knew I was up against it complaining about a solicitor,' says Irene. 'I was delighted to win my case – the verdict was more important than the damages.'
© *Bella*
January, 1997

20 sure-fire stress beaters

By Jane Alexander

Ask the next six people you see if they feel stressed and we bet five (if not all) of them will say yes. And come to think of it, you've been feeling irritable and put upon lately too, haven't you? Stress is something we see as a badge of courage for surviving the late 20th century. It makes us feel important. It can also be a health hazard. Researchers believe it's not only how we respond to stress now that affects our bodies and brains, but how we responded to stress in the past. Experts in the US say that we may respond to stress as we do to an allergy, becoming overly sensitive to stressful situations. 'This sensitisation actually alters the physical patterns in the brain,' says Seymour Levine of the University of Delaware. Which means next time we get stressed, 'We produce too many excitatory chemicals or too few calming ones; both inappropriate responses.' So what's the answer? Mastering as many anti-stress techniques as possible now – so that you avoid reaching your pressure point altogether. Here's our list of the 20 best, most effective stress stoppers.

Screaming, punching, boxing

Do these all sound too good to be true? Well, Dr Malcolm Rigler, a family GP from the West Midlands, advises stressed patients to act out their frustrations in a physical (but completely harmless) manner – smashing old plates on the floor or flinging a rubber brick against the wall. Stress experts agree that releasing tension and anger in a controlled environment can set free the stress hormones that are rampaging around our bodies – thereby promoting a feeling of relaxation. As Robert Holden, author of *Stress Busters* (Thorsons, £6.99), advises, 'Laugh it out, cry it out or scream it out. Learning to relax, to release and let go is a veritable art.'

Exercising

Like it or not, studies have shown that a 15-minute walk is more effective at dealing with stress than a course of tranquillisers. However, sports psychologist Christopher Connolly recommends hard aerobic exercise for stress release. He explains that we often become 'stuck in the twilight zone' where we've become 'aroused' through the stress of the day but are unable to release the body's raging stress hormones. 'Good hard exercise can allow you to swing back into the state we know as rest,' he says.

Floating

Forget images of blissed-out hippies – visiting your local floatation tank (sensory deprivation in a soundproof tank containing about half a metre of saline water) provides a highly effective means of relaxation and the chance to completely zone out for an hour. Neuroendocrinologist John Turner and psychologist Thomas Fine tested the effects of floating on hormones and other neuro-chemicals. They discovered that even a single float could activate the relaxation response, and that a series of floats had a strong 'maintenance effect'.

Autogenic training

A series of mental exercises designed to switch off the 'fight or flight' response – AT might sound rather technical, but actually it's dead easy and hugely successful. Extensively researched, it's now used to reduce stress and improve performance. Dr Malcolm Carruthers, who's spent his life researching stress, is convinced that AT is a large part of the answer. 'It's a bit like a westernised form of meditation,' he says. 'But it doesn't demand any belief systems. I like to call it mental circuit training.' Try it: sit in a chair with your hands resting on your arms, and give yourself relaxing instructions – 'My right hand is heavy, my arms and legs are heavy . . .' You can use the exercises at any time – even in the office or on the bus.

Biofeedback

Another scientific-sounding one, but biofeedback has been used for 50 years by doctors, psychologists and nurses to help people cope with stress. There are three main forms: electromyography (EMG), galvanic skin response (GSR) and electroencephalography (EEG). By attaching electrodes to a body system that readily reacts to stress (your muscles, skin and brain waves respectively), biofeedback allows you to monitor how stressed you are and teaches you to control – and even reduce – stress. The biofeedback machines give off a signal, generally a blinking light or a sound tone, that tells you your stress levels are high – all you have to do is concentrate on slowing the light or reducing the sound.

Mind machines

Virtual reality at its simplest, these machines make it possible to alter the frequency of the electrical impulses in your brain by flashing lights at precise speeds and rhythms. The brain picks up the frequency in a process known as 'entertainment'. Put your brain in the right rhythm and it becomes easy to drop into a state of deep relaxation. Mind machines consist of headphones and goggles attached to a control box and are being used in medical establishments in Germany. For more information contact Life Tools, tel: 01625 502602.

Deep breathing

When we're stressed we breathe more swiftly and shallowly, higher up in the chest. So it makes sense that deep abdominal breathing can help us relax. To make sure you're breathing deeply, place one hand on your abdomen. Breathe in slowly through your nose and, as you do, you should feel your abdomen (rather than your chest) rise. As you breathe out, your abdomen should fall.

Adaptogens

Herbs known as adaptogens are superb foot soldiers in the battle against stress. Researchers at the University of Munich defined adaptogens as 'substances meant to put the organism into a state of nonspecific heightened resistance in order to better fend off stresses and adapt to extraordinary challenges'. In particular, check out Siberian ginseng. Clinical trials on humans indicated that Siberian ginseng had precise effects on their ability to withstand stress. Others include panax ginseng and pfaffia – a Brazilian plant used for centuries as a tonic.

Listening to music

Tests have shown that half an hour of classical music is as effective as a dose of Valium. The ultimate stress-reducing soundwaves come from the PRE (Profound Relaxation Experience) Table, which sends sound waves through a special kind of water bed vibrating up through the entire body. At Lynden Hill Clinic in Berkshire, a centre for medical and surgical rehabilitation, the bed is used to reduce the physiological responses to stress. 'We use specific tapes of vibrational frequency music in conjunction with the bed that directly affect the central nervous system,' says Carole Easton. Failing that, put on your favourite mellowing-out music, sit back and relax.

Chi kung

Chi kung combines breathing techniques with precise movements and mental concentration. Clinical psychologist Kaleghl Quinn combines chi kung with martial arts, self-defence, assertiveness training and deep relaxation techniques in a stress-busting package called Quindo, which is so successful that Quinn works with several businesses to beat stress in the workplace. Contact The Quindo Centre and Clinic, tel: 0181 455 8698.

Bubble wrap

A curious but scientifically tested instant stress reliever. Dr Kathleen Dillon, professor of psychology at Western New England College in Massachusetts, USA, found that students felt far less tense and stressed after popping sheets of the wrap. This rather bizarre therapy works, says Dr Dillon, because it dispels pent-up nervous energy and muscle tension. She points out that manipulating or touching objects is a great relaxant (hence worry beads).

Meditation

Perhaps the best long-term stress solution going. Stress researcher Dr Herbert Benson, of Harvard Medical School, USA, found that while the 'fight or flight' reaction to stress is triggered by the sympathetic nervous system, its opposite – the para-sympathetic nervous system – works by decreasing muscular tension and releasing biochemicals that fill the body with a sense of relaxation, pleasure, wellbeing and safety. He called it the 'Relaxation Response' and found that meditation was probably the most effective means of provoking this response. Sit quietly, breathe deeply and keep focusing on your breathing rather than your thoughts. Aim for ten to 20 minutes a day.

Visualisation

Imagining yourself in a calm, beautiful place is one of the key strategies suggested by stress experts. 'Visualise lying on a beach,' advises Dr Paul Rosch, president of the American Institute of Stress. 'Listen to the waves and feel the warm sun and gentle breezes on your back.' Ursula Markham, stress expert and author of Managing Stress (Element, £6.99), advises conjuring up an image of a special place where you can feel comfortable and safe. 'Simply

bringing it to mind will be sufficient to have a calming influence upon you and your life.'

Yoga

Godfrey Devereux, who teaches yoga at London's Life Centre, says it's a supreme stress buster. 'You're not just working on the anatomical body but on the nervous system as well,' he says. Unlike more athletic forms of exercise you're not pumping the muscles but stretching them, taking the blood deeper into the cells of the tissues to oxygenate them and remove tensions along with any toxins.

Aromatherapy

One of the most luxurious ways of stress busting. According to aromatherapist Valerie Ann Worwood, author of *The Fragrant Mind* (Doubleday, £15.99), 'Essential oils may provide the most successful way of coping with the problems associated with and caused by stress.' She pinpoints eucalyptus lemon, which appears to boost the immune system and soothe the brain. Others include lavender, geranium, Roman camomile, sandalwood and mandarin. Olfactory researcher Professor George Dodd also found that he could soothe deep stress simply by asking subjects to sniff various compounds. One compound, Osmone 1 (apparently a blend of armpit sweat and secretions from the mammary glands), reduced stress symptoms by 50 per cent. It's said to replicate the smell a baby receives from its mother.

Nutrition

Dull as it sounds, diet is crucial in beating stress. 'One of the things that most subjects your body to negative stress is eating the wrong kinds of foods,' says health expert Lesley Kenton. Try to cut out or down on all refined carbohydrates and sugar; tea and coffee; sweetened commercial drinks; highly processed and junk foods; excess fat and preservatives. Boost your diet with fresh vegetables and fruits; wholegrain breads, pastas and cereals; pulses, nuts and oats. Eat foods rich in potassium, but low in sodium, for example potatoes, tomatoes, bananas, oranges, apples, chicken, cod and salmon.

Start delegating both at work and at home

Supplements

Experts at Solgar Vitamins point out that vitamins and minerals can play a supporting role in stress relief – you also need to learn relaxation techniques, exercise more and eat a healthy diet. Adequate levels of potassium are essential. The B vitamins and vitamin C 'have significant stress-reducing properties to a great extent because of their beneficial effect on the function of the adrenal gland, the body's stress regulator'. The minerals zinc, calcium and magnesium also help by reducing nervous irritability, muscle tension and hypertension.

Progressive relaxation

Try this simple technique to help your relaxation response kick in. Focus on each major muscle group in the body in turn. The muscle is contracted forcefully for one to two seconds, then allowed to relax. Start with the face and neck, then the muscles of the upper arms and chest followed by the lower arms and hands. Proceed down the body. Repeat the whole process two or three times. Experts advise you put aside five to ten minutes a day to reap the best benefits.

Massage

Tiffany Field has conducted extensive research into the power of touch at the Touch Research Institute at the University of Miami, USA. Tests showed that after a series of massages people felt better, less anxious and more in control. It wasn't just the feel-good factor either. 'Biochemicals associated with anxiety – cortisol and norepinephrine – decreased,' says Field. Further studies reinforced the message. Office workers who underwent two 15-minute massages a week found they had less fatigue, could think more clearly and had fewer symptoms of stress.

Delegate

Face it, you're not superhuman. Even the biggest control freak can't do it all. Virtually every stress management consultant would tell you to get your priorities straight – your health is more important than anything else. 'Start delegating both at work and at home,' urges Lesley Kenton. 'So many people assume they're supposed to be able to do everything,' she says. 'You're not. You're human.' Dr George F Solomon, a psychiatrist and pioneer in the field of psychoneurimmunology, the study of mind-body, agrees that we need to learn to say no. There's no doubt, he warns, that when we allow ourselves to be dragged into a role or activity to please others we'll end up stressed.

© *New Woman*
June, 1996

Lie back and enjoy your vices, say scientists

By Sarah Boseley

The British are a pleasure-loving nation, revelling in sex, music, wine, chocolate and the odd cigar, but are undermining their health by feeling guilty about it, scientists claimed yesterday.

David Warburton, head of Psychopharmacology at Reading University, claimed that pleasure, in moderation, was good for health – and guilt is not.

In a survey of European attitudes compiled by Professor Warburton, the United Kingdom came second in the pleasure league, but third in the guilt league out of eight countries where attitudes were polled. Most laid-back were the Dutch, who enjoyed themselves the most, and felt the least guilt.

Professor Warburton is founder of a group of some 60 scientists worldwide with the tongue-in-cheek acronym of Arise – the Association for Research into the Science of Enjoyment. But the science is serious, he says. Enjoyment relieves stress and enhances the immune system, they have found, while guilt is potentially damaging.

'In its extreme, guilt can impair attentiveness, making people forgetful and more prone to error,' he said. 'Chronic guilt can induce stress and depression which could lead to eating disorders and contribute to infection, ulcers, heart problems and even brain damage.

'A number of common pleasures – such as eating chocolate and sweet things, smoking and lack of exercise – have attracted high levels of guilt, perhaps reflecting the high profile of health campaigns which have affected the way people view their pleasures. People should not feel guilty about pleasure-giving activities, as long as they don't over-indulge or harm others.'

Few people feel guilty about those pleasures which have not been condemned by the health lobby, such as sex and listening to music. Interestingly, while on average sex rated as the second most pleasurable activity across the eight nations, in the UK it topped the table, largely put there by the vote of the women.

Those activities people feel most guilty about are the lack of sport and exercise, cakes and ice cream, smoking and eating chocolate. In the 'second division' of guilt-inducing pleasures come beer, wine and spirits, shopping for pleasure, TV and videos. In the third division are red meat, sex, cheese, cream and butter, eating out and tea and coffee. Least guilt-inducing is listening to music. Professor Warburton says he and his fellow scientists are not in the pocket of any lobbying or commercial organisation. Arise advocates moderation in all things – a little of what you fancy, in fact.

© *The Guardian*
November, 1996

A little of what you fancy...

Study of enjoyment of various activities (including listening to music, sex, eating out, smoking) and the guilt associated with these activities. Eight selected countries

Pleasure experienced (maximum 130)
Guilt experienced (maximum 100)

Country	Pleasure	Guilt
Netherlands	89.6	12.9
UK	86.6	22.8
Australia	84.7	27.2
Italy	84.1	20.1
Switzerland	83.9	22.7
Belgium	83.4	19.2
Spain	81.6	20.1
Germany	79.0	24.5

Source: Arise

Stress – why does it happen?

By Dr R J Wycherley

Life is not a smooth path, it throws up a succession of problems, large and small, which make demands on us; getting to work on time, getting through household chores, coping with heavy traffic, getting over bereavement, under-going redundancy and so on. This list could be endless and the problems keep coming at us; that's what life is like. Demands can also come from inside ourselves; we may feel we have to live our lives in particular ways which put pressure on us. For example, we may feel that we must help others, and consequently we may take on too much and become overloaded.

To deal with life's demands, we have three allies:

- *Skills* we have learned – such as driving, sewing, communication with others, or using computers;
- *Resources inside* – such as good health, stamina, intelligence or emotional expressiveness;
- *Resources outside* – such as income, good friends, somewhere to live, libraries or people who have the technical skills we need.

Imagine your skills and resources as being like stock in a storeroom, which you can draw on when life's demands come up. You can select the right mix of skills and resources to deal with whatever problem faces you. Some situations need advice from others, some need strength, some need the ability to sew, and so on. In our minds, we constantly weigh up the demands life makes on us against the stock of skills and resources we have available.

If we have more than we need to solve the problem facing us, we will carry on with life without experiencing much in the way of stress. When we have only just enough skills and resources to cope with the demand on us, we feel challenged – but also invigorated, we know we can get by but it will take some effort. People frequently place themselves in situations where their skills and resources are stretched because they like the feeling of being challenged. Rock climbers, racing drivers or soldiers are just some examples of this.

But what happens if the demands on us exceed our stock of skills and resources? Then we become 'stressed'. We are not sure we can cope, and may become overwhelmed. Our bodies begin to switch into 'red alert', our minds fill with thoughts of disaster, and we know we have to fight, run, or stay still and be harmed. Imagine you are crossing a busy road with fast traffic. You reach the middle and notice a car approaching you very fast. If you don't move quickly you may be breathing your last. Imagine you are sixteen, in the peak of health and fitness. You have brilliant hearing and vision, superb reflexes and are a champion sprinter. Would you feel stressed by the approaching car? Probably not – you'd simply run out of the way, your skills and resources are well able to deal with the demand on you. Now imagine you are an elderly person who needs a stick to walk. Your hearing and vision are not good and it takes you longer to notice the approaching car. You know you can't run, in fact you can't even walk very quickly. Would you feel stressed? You certainly would! You know you don't have the skills and resources to deal with the problem and you realise that your life depends on the driver seeing you in time.

What if we can't fight, or run, and the situation doesn't go away? In this case we may remain physically on 'red alert' for long periods of time, and may be more susceptible to illness because of this. So what can we do to manage stress better? Firstly, we need to accept that life is like a choppy sea

and always will be. Life continually presents us with opportunities to learn and change and we can become stronger by doing so. We can learn to control the demands on us; identify situations which are stressful and work out how to manage them better. Anticipating stressful situations and planning ahead means allowing for extra time, sleep, help, and so on. Work out your key goals in life and begin pruning unnecessary activities. Time management is vital; give time to your key goals, let minor things remain undone, delegate, say no to people who will steal your time, don't put things off, do them now!

Learn skills which will help you and have an attitude that you will keep learning as long as you are alive. Value your mistakes as opportunities to understand what you do wrong and learn from them. Some useful skills are:

- Practical 'how to do it' skills – such as cooking, plumbing or writing letters;
- Caring for yourself – liking yourself, looking after yourself physically, enjoying your body, being friends with yourself;
- Managing the physical aspects of stress – learning a skill such as relaxation, yoga, meditation, or exercise (such as aerobics, dancing, jogging, juggling);
- Being assertive – knowing and saying what you want, expressing feelings, both positive and negative, clearly;
- Problem solving – learning how to define problems clearly and produce possible solutions;
- Negotiating – learning to negotiate with others as an equal adult; putting your case, listening to others, reaching conclusions that are mutually satisfactory;
- Developing a 'philosophy' or spiritual basis for your life – this can guide your actions and help you work out the right course to take.

Finally, build up and use your resources. These include access to information, advice, support, and technical skills. Try to build up a support network of people on whom you can call. Learn how to ask for help, and to be helped, and to swap help with others.

• Dr R J Wycherley is senior clinical psychologist at the Hastings & Rother NHS Trust

© 1996 OpenMind, reprinted from OpenMind 81 (Sept/Oct 1996)) by permission of Mind (National Association for Mental Health)

Time to talk

**Call The Samaritans, 24 hours a day, 7 days a week.
Every single day of the year. We're always there to listen**

We listen

It doesn't matter who you are, if you're in crisis, despairing or suicidal it can make all the difference to talk about how you are feeling.

Because problems can get on top of anyone. Men and women. Gay and straight. Any religion and colour. Any age.

You can talk to us about anything that is troubling you: we will not judge you; we will not tell you what to do, but we will try to help you think things through; we will listen with an open mind for as long as you need.

You can speak in total confidence to one of our volunteers. They come from all walks of life and every kind of background. All are carefully trained to listen.

Just call

You can call us anytime – night or day – every day of the year.

If you need to talk to someone face to face, you can visit one of over 200 Branches across the UK and Ireland.

You can write to us, or even send us an e-mail.

We always have time for you – 24 hours a day

Make contact

Phone us
0345 90 90 90 for the cost of a local call.

All Branches can be telephoned day or night, 7 days a week including Bank Holidays. Or find our local number in the phone book, Yellow Pages or ask the Operator.

Visit one of our Branches
All our Branches are open to callers, and can be visited any day or evening. Many Branches have disabled access.

Write to us
You can write to any Branch, they will all reply to letters.

And there is a Correspondence Branch (for letters only) at: PO Box 9, Stirling, Scotland.

Chris, PO Box 1250, Slough SL1 1ST (for people in prison or on remand).

Send us an e-mail
You can e-mail us on the Internet at: jo@samaritans.org or (anonymously): samaritans@anon.penet.fi

Contact us by text phone
We have two national text phone numbers: 0181 780 2521 and 01204 31122 and several branches have text phones.

The Samaritans is a nationwide charity providing confidential emotional support to anyone in crisis. We are not a religious or political organisation, and rely mainly on donations from the public. For general information, please write to: The Samaritans, 10 The Grove, Slough SL1 1QP.

© The Samaritans

Changing your life

An extract from *The Which? Guide to Managing Stress*

Terminally ill people soon realise that time cannot be squandered. They realise that they have little time left to fulfil their hopes, dreams and ambitions. Patients respond to the intense stress of impending death in different ways. They may quit their jobs to spend more time with their families. They may renew their interest in their careers. They may paint, write poetry or visit places they always wanted to see. But why wait until you face death to do these things? You can reduce stress by changing your life now.

Identify your problem

The first step is to understand your stress. But identifying the cause of your stress is often more difficult than it seems. Often we know that something is wrong but we have only a vague idea of why. We may be unhappy at work. We may feel unsatisfied with life generally. However, we rarely take the time to try to understand the cause of our distress. So on a blank piece of paper, write the following headings:

- What is the problem?
- Who is the problem?
- Where does the problem occur?
- Why does the problem occur?
- When does the problem occur?

If answering these questions does not reveal a specific cause for your anxiety, keep a diary for a fortnight. You can either keep the classic journal and record your thoughts and impressions each day, or you can simply note what you are doing or thinking about each time you feel tense, stressed or anxious. This can provide you with an insight into your problems. You might also consider counselling or psycho-therapy. A trained outside observer can offer a new perspective that helps you get to the root of your problems.

Diaries can also help you tackle specific problems. So, if you want to cut down the amount of alcohol you consume, keep a record for a couple of weeks of when, where and how much you drink. Keeping a record means you have a target to aim at and should reveal ways you can change your habits.

Our quizzes on the next page should also give you some insight into the severity of your stress and whether stress has begun to spill over into anxiety or depression.

So how can you assess how stressed you are at the moment? One way is to count the number of stress signals you experience.

How many stress signals do you experience?

The wide variation in our response to stress – and our coping strategies – is reflected in the range of stress-related symptoms. The more of these stress signals you experience, the more serious your stress problem. However, the stress signals may change from moment to moment, so it may be better to note how many symptoms you experience over 24 hours.

Stress signals

- headaches
- muscle tension; stiff neck
- feeling isolated
- changed eating habits
- palpitations; rapid heart beat
- feeling scared
- sleep disturbances; insomnia
- fatigue
- crying for no reason
- breathing problems
- grinding teeth
- feeling of impending doom
- pallor
- inability to forget problems
- diarrhoea; constipation
- feeling pressurised
- nervousness; anxiety
- irritability; anger
- feeling jumpy; racing apprehensive thoughts
- procrastination; worry about making the wrong decision
- increased smoking or drinking
- being brusque, rude or sarcastic
- sexual problems; impotence
- losing interest in your hobbies or job
- poor concentration
- a 'lump' in your throat
- cold hands or feet; excessive sweating; a 'cold sweat'
- weak knees; dizziness; feeling faint
- excessively sensitive to outside stimuli
- muscle twitches and tics
- preoccupied with misfortune
- 'butterflies' in the stomach; nausea; indigestion/dyspepsia

Are you anxious or depressed?

Everyone is anxious at one time or another. But how do you know if your stress has triggered a more serious problem such as chronic anxiety or depression? Doctors commonly use the Hospital Anxiety and Depression Scale to distinguish the two conditions. However, remember that most depressed people also suffer from anxiety and that psychiatric conditions are notoriously difficult to self-diagnose. After all, you're using the same organ that is supposed to be ill to diagnose that something's wrong.

• The above is an extract from *The Which? Guide to Managing Stress*, by Mark Greener, ISBN 0 85202 608 0 priced at £9.99. Published by Which? Books.   © 1996 Which? Ltd

Anxiety and depression quiz

Complete both tests below, ideally when you've had a 'normal' day rather than an intensely stressful or relaxing one. Check your score below. If you score more than eight then you may be suffering from these problems. The closer your score to eight, the stronger your depressive or anxious trait. In other words, if you score six or seven, doctors may not regard you as suffering from anxiety yet, but you're well on your way. If you score eight or more you may want to consult your doctor, especially if you've had the symptoms for more than a month.

Anxiety quiz

1. *I feel tense or wound up*
(a) Most of the time
(b) A lot of the time
(c) From time to time, occasionally
(d) Not at all

2. *I get a sort of frightened feeling as if something awful is about to happen*
(a) Very definitely and quite badly
(b) Yes, but not too badly
(c) A little, but it doesn't worry me
(d) Not at all

3. *Worrying thoughts go through my mind*
(a) A great deal of the time
(b) A lot of the time
(c) From time to time, not too often
(d) Only occasionally

4. *I can sit at ease and feel relaxed*
(a) Definitely
(b) Usually
(c) Not often
(d) Not at all

5. *I get a sort of frightened feeling like 'butterflies' in the stomach*
(a) Not at all
(b) Occasionally
(c) Quite often
(d) Very often

6. *I feel restless as if I have to be on the move*
(a) Very much indeed
(b) Quite a lot
(c) Not very much
(d) Not at all

7. *I get sudden feelings of panic*
(a) Very often indeed
(b) Quite often
(c) Not very often
(d) Not at all

Depression quiz

1. *I still enjoy the things I used to enjoy*
(a) Definitely as much
(b) Not quite so much
(c) Only a little
(d) Hardly at all

2. *I can laugh and see the funny side of things*
(a) As much as I always could
(b) Not quite so much now
(c) Definitely not so much now
(d) Not at all

3. *I feel cheerful*
(a) Not at all
(b) Not often
(c) Sometimes
(d) Most of the time

4. *I feel as if I am slowed down*
(a) Nearly all the time
(b) Very often
(c) Sometimes
(d) Not at all

5. *I have lost interest in my appearance*
(a) Definitely
(b) I don't take as much care
(c) I may not take quite as much care
(d) I take just as much care as ever

6. *I look forward with enjoyment to things*
(a) As much as ever I did
(b) Rather less than I used to
(c) Definitely less than I used to
(d) Hardly at all

7. *I can enjoy a good book or radio or TV programme*
(a) Often
(b) Sometimes
(c) Not often
(d) Very seldom

Scores

Anxiety scores: **Q1.** (a)3 (b)2 (c)1 (d)0, **Q2.** (a)3 (b)2 (c)1 (d)0, **Q3.** (a)3 (b)2 (c)1 (d)0, **Q4.** (a)0 (b)1 (c)2 (d)3, **Q5.** (a)0 (b)1 (c)2 (d)3, **Q6.** (a)3 (b)2 (c)1 (d)0, **Q7.** (a)3 (b)2 (c)1 (d)0.

Depression scores: **Q1.** (a)0 (b)1 (c)2 (d)3, **Q2.** (a)0 (b)1 (c)2 (d)3, **Q3.** (a)3 (b)2 (c)1 (d)0, **Q4.** (a)3 (b)2 (c)1 (d)0, **Q5.** (a)3 (b)2 (c)1 (d)0, **Q6.** (a)0 (b)1 (c)2 (d)3, **Q7.** (a)0 (b)1 (c)2 (d)3.

- The above is an extract from *The Which? Guide to Managing Stress*, by Mark Greener, ISBN 0 85202 608 0 priced at £9.99. Published by Which? Books.

© 1996 Which? Ltd

Anti-stress room is a smash hit

By Jonathan Watts in Tokyo

'At first I wasn't sure if I ought to. After all, everything was so valuable. But once I got started... well, I just let rip and it felt fantastic.'

When Mr Watanabe, who describes himself as an ordinary Japanese businessman, and three of his female colleagues entered the stress-relief room it resembled a tiny antiques shop. Gilt-framed paintings hung on the walls, an elaborately decorated screen stood in a corner, and statuettes and an ornate Imari vase were neatly arranged on a mother-of-pearl table top.

Two hours later, Mr Watanabe and friends left the place looking as if it had been hit by a typhoon. The frames were mangled, the pictures torn, the screen chipped, the table wrecked, the statuettes headless and smithereens of the vase lay scattered on the floor.

'Mr Watanabe is a good customer,' said the owner, Yoshie Ogasawara, as she surveyed the destruction. 'Some of the others can get carried away. It takes days to clean up after them.'

The stress-relief room, in the tranquil surroundings of a small lakeside town at the foot of Mount Fuji, was set up by Ms Ogasawara in July. For 10,000 yen (about £52), you get the use of the room for two hours. This includes as much beer as you can drink, as many karaoke songs as you can sing and as much havoc as you can wreak.

'Everyone gets stressed out occasionally,' Ms Ogasawara explained, 'but perhaps especially so in Japan. Here people are expected to keep up appearances whatever they are feeling inside. This room is a way for them to let off steam.'

While smashing the room, middle-ranking managers have been heard screaming abuse at their seniors, housewives cursing their unfaithful husbands and bureaucrats ridiculing their political superiors. One customer wrote to Ms Ogasawara after a smashing session: 'I can't thank you enough. You have made me look at things in a new light.'

> For 10,000 yen, about £52, you get the use of the room for two hours. This includes as much beer as you can drink, as many karaoke songs as you can sing and as much havoc as you can wreak

It might be good therapy, but even with five customers at a time entry fees fail to cover the £1,000 value of the goods that get demolished.

Ms Ogasawara said she was not worried. 'During the bubble economy of the 1980s there was a glut of everything in Japan – money and goods. But now that prices have fallen and people have gone bust I have been able to pick up stuff at a bargain.

'Some customers ask me to let then take some of the objects away with them, but that is not the point. I don't want people to hoard things that should be enjoyed, even if that means smashing them.'

The end of December is traditionally a time for *bonenkai* ('forget the year') parties, an opportunity for Japanese to unwind and put the frustrations of the previous twelve months behind them. Fully booked for the season, the stress-relief room is being restocked for the coming orgy of non-gratuitous violence.

© *The Guardian*
November, 1996

Help! I haven't got time for my life

When was the last time you had a moment to yourself? Are you so busy that you never really feel relaxed? And if you do get the chance to snatch a few minutes to yourself, do you feel racked with guilt?

If so, you could be risking your physical and psychological well-being, according to Briton Nick Williams, a personal development consultant.

'Lack of so-called quality time can spark headaches, stomach upsets and skin problems,' he says.

In the Eighties, time management courses focused on fitting as much into one day as possible. However, the Nineties version is more about learning to pare down your schedule to take time out for yourself.

Nick suggests planning refreshment breaks – points in your day you use to regenerate yourself, setting aside at least two 15 minute periods when you can go for a short walk, take a breath of fresh air, read an inspiring book, or simply close your eyes and relax.

'Life is more a marathon than a sprint,' he says, 'so you have to learn how to pace yourself if you're going to get through it.' To examine Nick's claims, Self publishes some essential tips on how to make more time and looks at the lives of three busy women whose time management needs improving.

How to make time

Take a pen or pencil and a piece of paper, draw a large rectangular shape and then divide it into four equal squares. Think of tasks you have to do and then prioritise them by placing them in the appropriate square.

A top right (for tasks that are urgent and important).
B top left (for tasks that are urgent but not important).
C bottom right (for tasks that are important but not urgent).
D bottom left (for tasks that are neither urgent nor important).

Once you've done that, act accordingly. Things in category A you should do immediately; those in both B and C you ought to do at some point in the near future. Square D is your dumping ground for tasks that are not pressing – ignore these for the time being.

The time graph

In order to take control over your time, Patsy Westcott, author of *How To Get What You Want* (Bloomsbury, £6.99) suggests plotting out a graph.

Take a piece of paper and write the hours of the day along the top and the days of the week down the left hand side. Note how you spend your time, breaking it down into ten-minute intervals and record each task, event or pastime on your chart.

At the end of the week take hold of three different coloured pencils or crayons and colour as follows. Red: time spent doing things that you really enjoyed. Yellow: time spent doing things you moderately enjoyed. Blue: time spent doing things that gave you no satisfaction whatsoever. Taking everything into consideration, see if there are any ways you can do less of the activities that are coloured blue and more of the ones coloured red.

'Time management is simply the art of arranging your time so that you spend it doing what you want rather than being at the mercy of others and events over which you have no control,' says Patsy.

- If you're busy, keep the answerphone switched on. Devote a chunk of time to returning your calls.
- Invest in a diary or a Filofax so you can plan your time properly.
- Make a list. As well as all the things you've got to do, always try to include one or two 'treats' for today.

I feel uneasy if I ever relax

Jocelyn Readman, 37, lives in Surrey with her husband Steve, 38, a company director, and her three children: Amy, eight, Ella, six, Robert, four. Her day begins at 7am and she only finds time for herself after 8pm.

Looking after three children and organising a family leaves me with virtually no time to myself. I get up at seven to make breakfast and after getting the children dressed, we walk to school. Then I do a bit of housework.

At 11.50am I collect Robert from school, make lunch and at 3pm it's back to school again to collect the girls, when I chat to other mums. This is my usual daily pattern except for Wednesday mornings when I help run a reading group for eight and nine year olds.

Out of school time is usually taken up with organising the children's lives. Amy goes to ballet classes after school, so I have to prepare the evening meal around that. All the children are in bed about eight, depending on whether they've got homework.

Steve earns the money, while I do everything around the house. He has a demanding job so I shield him from as much stress as possible.

Before I became a mother, I worked as a home economist and had dreams of having time to bake elaborate cakes. Unfortunately, the reality is different and I find I depend on convenience foods. There are a host of things I would like to do if I had the time – go to the theatre or the cinema and pamper myself by going for a sauna. Even finding the time to have my hair cut is difficult.

Running a home and looking after a husband and children means that my priorities usually come bottom of the list. I'm not complaining. This is my career and I'm committed to bringing up my family. But sometimes I yearn for more time for myself.

The problem is that a lot of women who stay at home feel terribly guilty if they take time out for themselves. I know that sometimes if I make coffee and settle down to day-time television I feel uneasy. At the back of my mind I think I should be turning out cupboards or cleaning the kitchen floor.

Nick Williams' advice
Jocelyn needs to overcome her guilt. She might feel happier and more energetic. She should also learn to say 'No' to extra responsibilities – self-worth is not simply tied up with what we do for others. She should keep in mind that we accomplish the great task by a series of small acts.

> *Busy lives can be fulfilling just as long as we take time out to renew, refresh and enjoy life for ourselves. Balance is the key*

I suggest she snatches some time for herself between picking up Robert and returning to school at 3pm. She could easily find the opportunity to sit down and relax. And after she's put the children to bed, she could closet herself into a room or run herself a relaxing bath.

No break for lunch if the job is non-stop

Jo Campbell, 29, an executive personal assistant at WEA Records, lives in Farnham, Surrey. Divorced, she shares her home with her boyfriend, Chris, 28, and her five-year old son, Dale.

I have no time to myself during the week. I get up at 6.45am, make my son's breakfast and then shoot out to catch a train to London. Then I travel across London and I'm usually at my desk by 9.30am.

No two days are the same as my job involves co-ordinating video directors and photographers, organising meetings and dealing with recording artists. I never have time to nip out of the office at lunchtime – if I do it's only to get a sandwich, which I then eat at my desk.

It really is a non-stop job, and I never get the chance to leave the office until seven or eight in the evening. Then I have to face a two-hour journey back to Surrey.

By the time I get home my son is usually asleep and during the week I never really have the opportunity to spend time with him. I resent this and often feel I'm a terrible mother. But at the moment I don't have much choice. I like my job and I need to work in order to help support us.

In the evenings, I eat, watch the late news and then drop into bed by about 11.30. I wish I could spend more time with my son and my boyfriend, Chris, and I would like to go shopping, do some exercise, or have a social life.

Fortunately my weekends are undemanding. I catch up on my sleep and spend time with Dale. I take him to the cinema, McDonald's or out for a walk in the countryside. But having a child and working means that even then there's not much time left for me.

I spend up to five hours a day commuting to a demanding job – during which I read papers, magazines and chat to friends on my mobile – and then I've got a child to look after as well. If it weren't for the fact that Chris takes Dale to school and looks after him during the day and early evening, I wouldn't know what to do. I can't really see any solution to the problem. I accept that at this point in time my needs have to come last.

Nick Williams' advice
I would suggest that Jo gets up at 6.30 so she could do 15 minutes of gentle stretching exercises. She should also use the commuting time to practise relaxation techniques to keep her balanced during stressful periods.

I also think that she should carve out an hour over the weekend which is just for her. Instead of dropping into bed in the evenings, she could take a 15-minute bath with relaxing aromatherapy oils to help her sleep.

Busy lives can be fulfilling just as long as we take time out to renew, refresh and enjoy life for ourselves. Balance is the key.

Jo should make herself a proper lunch break. If she really can't, she should go for a 15-minute walk, or grab a few minutes for herself mid-afternoon. It's all very well having a demanding job, but she really won't function to her best if she carries on with this routine.

© *The Daily Mail October, 1996*

Phoney smile at work will end in tears

Flare-ups may be all the rage, but hiding your feelings can be worse

By Andrew Loudon

People who mask their true feelings at work may be furthering their career at the expense of their health.

Faking enthusiasm and interest while hiding anger, disappointment and boredom causes huge stress, says a study reported yesterday. And it can increase the risk of heart disease.

Television presenters such as Eamonn Holmes, who admitted his loathing for co-host Anthea Turner only after she left the GMTV breakfast show, top the false-front league, said research psychologist Sandi Mann.

'They are having to hide how they really feel all the time,' she said. 'Television must be the most extreme case. I watch Richard Madeley and Judy Finnigan and can only imagine the emotion management that must go on there when they have the whole country watching them.'

Miss Mann, from the University of Salford, told a British Psychological Society conference in Blackpool of the ways in which employees learn what is expected of them.

Major service industries such as McDonald's and Disneyland issue a written code. 'You have to smile and be warm, friendly and polite at all times,' she said. 'At Disneyland they say you have to produce self-esteem enhancing emotions to make the guests feel good.'

In some cases, certain emotional standards 'go with the job'. Flight attendants are supposed to be friendly and cheerful, and funeral directors to be sombre. Lawyers are expected to appear aloof, doctors to show detached concern and nurses to be supportive.

Faking enthusiasm and interest while hiding anger, disappointment and boredom causes huge stress

The need to take a break from these roles leads in private to black humour at the expense of the passenger, mourner, client or patient, said Miss Mann. 'But it is not being cruel – it is a way of relieving stress.'

Most people, however, pick up their ideas of what is acceptable through unwritten protocols. 'As you become immersed in the culture you learn what is OK and what is not OK,' she said. 'It is like laughing out loud on a bus – you might wish to, but you know people will think you are strange so you don't.'

All this 'emotional labour' can, said Miss Mann, be useful. 'It is a good thing to manage emotion and fake enthusiasm and interest – I would rather people I was with did that than show complete boredom towards me.'

But both employees and management should be aware that such behaviour cannot be kept up indefinitely without leading to stress-related illness. 'Downtime breaks', spent away from stressful situations, are the answer, she said.

- Workers disciplined for breaking company rules often feel so resentful that they deliberately break some more, the conference was told.

In a study of 104 cases, only 24 per cent accepted that the rule they had broken had a good purpose, and another 30 per cent agreed only grudgingly to observe the rule in future. The rest felt so strongly they were 'victims of punishment' that the disciplinary procedure was counter-productive, claimed Dr Derek Rollinson, of the University of Huddersfield Business School. 'The trick is to get the person to admit guilt and start seeing the reason for the rule,' he said. 'It comes down to poor handling by managers.'

© *The Daily Mail* January, 1997

INDEX

absenteeism, and workplace stress 12, 17, 18
adolescents *see* young people
age, and stress in young people 3-4, 5, 10
alcohol, and stress 2, 15, 16
anger, and stress 24-5
anxiety
    diagnosing 32
    quiz 33

boys
    and depression 10
brain damage, and stress 16-17
bullying, and workplace stress 18, 20-1

childhood abuse, and stress 17
children, experiencing problems at school 3-5

depression
    diagnosing 32
    quiz 33
    and suicide 22
    and young people 9-10
drugs, and young people 2

education, young people's aspirations 1
emotional labour 37
employers, and workplace stress 12, 13, 23
examination pressures, and young people 1, 3-5

families
    and student life 8
    and young people under stress 2, 7
    see also parents
Field, Tim 21
financial pressures, and workplace stress 18
floating, relieving stress by 26
friends, and young people under stress 2, 7
girls
    and depression 10
guilt, and pleasure 29

health and safety issues, and workplace stress 13

identity, changing as a student 8

infertility, and stress 17

life events
    and depression in young people 9, 10
    and stress 17, 23

magazines, and young people 2
managers, and workplace stress 13, 17-19, 23

massage 28
mature students 8
meditation 27
men, and workplace stress 18, 19, 21, 22
mental health, and young people 1-2
mind machines 27
money, and young people's aspirations 1
music, listening to 27
    as a pleasure 29
    and young people under stress 2, 7

nutrition 28

occupational groups
    and stress 16
    and suicide rates 22
opinion polls, on rage attacks 24

parents, pressure on young people 4, 5, 6-7
pleasure, importance of 29
pollution, young people's concern about 1

rage attacks 24-5
relaxation 28
road rage 24-5
role conflict, and workplace stress 15

schools, young people and stress 3-5, 10
sex, young people's attitude to 1
Siberian ginseng 27
stress
    alternative/complementary stress remedies 19
    and brain damage 16-17
    defining 12, 14-15
    and infertility 17
    skills and resources in management of 30-1

    symptoms of 15, 19, 32
    ways of beating 26-8
    Which? guide to managing 32
    see also workplace stress; young people
stress-relief room 34
Stressed Out (ChildLine report) 5
student life 8-9
suicidal feelings, young people and exam stress 5
suicide
    and depression 22
    and workplace stress 15

telephone counselling
    Careline 11
    ChildLine 3-5
    Workplace Bullying Advice Line 21
time management 35-6

women
    and alternative/complementary stress remedies 19
    occupation and suicide rates 22
    and rage attacks 24
    and workplace stress 18, 18-19, 21, 23
workplace stress 12-23
    and absenteeism 12, 17, 18
    and breaking company rules 37
    and bullying 18, 20-1
    costs of 12, 21, 22
    counselling services 13
    education programmes 13
    and emotional labour 37
    and employers 12, 13, 23
    factors in 12-13
    health and safety issues 13
    ill-health resulting from 23
    legal position 23
    and lifestyle stress 18-19
    and managers 13, 17-19, 23
    and role conflict 15
    and work relationships 12

yoga 19, 28
young people 1-11
    and depression 9-10
    and examination pressures 1, 3-5
    and rage attacks 24
    sex differences
        in dealing with problems 2
        and depression 10
    and student life 8-9

ADDITIONAL RESOURCES

Campaign Against Bullying at Work (CABAW)
MSF Centre
33-37 Moreland Street
London EC1V 8BB
Tel: 0171 505 3054
Fax: 0171 505 3030
Launched by the MSF Union in January 1996, the campaign meets at the House of Lords and aims to introduce legislation to outlaw bullying at work.

Careline
Cardinal Heenan Centre
326 High Road
Ilford
Essex IG1 1QP
Tel: 0181 514 5444
Careline provides confidential telephone counselling for children, young people and adults. They offer a service which provides instant telephone counselling to any individual on any issue.
Tel: 0181 514 1177 Mon-Fri:10am – 4pm and 7pm – 10pm.

ChildLine
2nd Floor Royal Mail Building
Studd Street
London N1 0QW
Tel: 0171 239 1000 (admin)
Fax: 0171 239 1001
ChildLine is the free, national helpline for children and young people in trouble or danger. It provides confidential phone counselling service for any child with any problem 24 hours a day. Children or young people can phone or write free of charge about problems of any kind. ChildLine, Freepost 1111, London, N1 0BR.
Freephone 0800 1111

Consumers' Association
Which? Books
2 Marylebone Road
London W1 4DF
Tel: 0171 486 5544
A research and policy organisation providing a vigorous and independent voice for domestic consumers in the UK.

European Foundation for the Improvement of Living and Working Conditions
Wyattville Road
Loughlinstown
Co. Dublin
Ireland
Tel: 00 353 1 204 3100
Fax: 00 353 1 282 6456

Health Education Authority
Hamilton House
Mabledon Place
London
WC2H 9TX
Tel: 0171 3833 833
Fax: 0171 387 0550
Provides free legal advice for people on all health issues, including stress. They produce a wide range of publications

Industrial Society
Robert Hyde House
48 Bryanston Square
London W1H 7LN
Tel: 0171 262 2401
Fax: 0171 724 3354
Produces range of booklets and information packs on all sorts of work related issues including: working mothers, racial and sexual harassment, smoking and alcohol policies. Their library includes a wide range of press cuttings and employment statistics.

Institute of Personnel and Development (IPD)
IPD House
Camp Road
London SW19 4UX
Tel: 0181 971 9000
Fax: 0181 263 3333

Mental Health Foundation
37 Mortimer Street
London W1N 7RJ
Tel: 0171 580 0145
Fax: 0171 631 3868
Objects are to prevent mental disorder wherever possible by funding and supporting research and educating people about the causes and effects of stress.

MIND
Granta House
15-19 Broadway
London E15 4BQ
Tel: 0181 519 2122
MIND is a leading mental health charity in England and Wales. They produce a wide range of advice leaflets (45p each), reports and books. Publications. Ask for their publications list. Also produce the magazine *Open Mind*

The Institute of Management
3rd Floor
2 Savoy Court
Strand
London WC2R 0EZ
Tel: 0171 497 0580
Fax: 0171 497 0463

The Samaritans
10 The Grove
Slough
London SL1 1QP
Tel: 01753 532713
Fax: 01753 819004
Deals with suicide-related issues.

The Suzy Lamplugh Trust
14 East Sheen Avenue
London SW14 8AS
Tel: 0181 392 1839
Fax: 0181 392 1830
For information on bullying, send an SAE to the Trust.

Workplace Bullying
PO Box 77
Wantage
Oxfordshire OX12 8YP
Tel: 01235 834548
Helpline for bullying at work.

Young Minds
Young Minds Newsletter
102-108 Clerkenwell Road
London EC1M 5SA
Tel: 0171 336 8445
Fax: 0171 336 8446
Young Minds, the national association for children's mental health. Produces a range of leaflets, reports, a magazinea and newsletters.

ACKNOWLEDGEMENTS

The publisher is grateful for permission to reproduce the following material.

While every care has been taken to trace and acknowledge copyright, the publisher tenders its apology for any accidental infringement or where copyright has proved untraceable. The publisher would be pleased to come to a suitable arrangement in any such case with the rightful owner.

Chapter One: Young people and stress

Mental health and young people, © Health Education Authority, October 1996, *Stressed out*, © ChildLine, *Exams make teenagers suicidal*, © The Independent, April 1996, *I nearly cracked up*, © Sugar and Radio One, *How to cope with the stress of student life*, © MIND, *The feel-bad factor*, © Young People Now, October 1996, *Are you worried? Are you under stress?*, © Careline.

Chapter Two: Stress at work

Stress at work, © Mental Health Foundation, *Stress in the workplace*, © European Foundation for the Improvement of Living and Working Conditions, *How stress at work could be shrinking your brain*, © The Daily Mail, August 1996, *Managing stress*, © Industrial Society, *Are managers under stress?*, © The Institute of Management, September 1996, *Why stress is breeding the office superbully*, © The Daily Mail, November 1996, *Workplace bullying may cost employers and state £12 billion a year*, © Tim Field, *The cost of stress*, © The Samaritans, *The legal position*, © Health and Safety Executive.

Chapter Three: Coping with stress

What makes you angry?, © Bella, January 1997, *20 sure-fire stress beaters*, © New Woman, June 1996, *Lie back and enjoy your vices*, © The Guardian, November 1996, *A little of what you fancy . . .*, © Arise, *Stress – why does it happen?*, © OpenMind, September/October 1996, *Time to talk*, © The Samaritans, *Changing your life*, © 1996 Which? Ltd, *Anxiety and depression quiz*, © 1996 Which? Ltd, *Anti-stress room is a smash hit*, © The Guardian, November 1996, *Help! I haven't got time for my life*, © The Daily Mail, October 1996, *Phoney smile at work will end in tears*, © The Daily Mail, October 1996.

Photographs and Illustrations

Pages 1, 2, 6, 11: Katherine Fleming/Folio Collective, pages 4, 8, 30: Andrew Smith / Folio Collective, pages 14, 19, 34: Ken Pyne.

Craig Donnellan
Cambridge
January, 1997